A Victorian Young Lady

A Victorian Young Lady

BETTY ASKWITH

MICHAEL RUSSELL

© Betty Askwith 1978

First published in Great Britain 1978
by Michael Russell (Publishing) Ltd
The Chantry, Wilton, Salisbury

Reprinted 1979

ISBN 0 85955 061 3

Printed by Hillman Printers (Frome) Ltd, Somerset

For K. M. J.

Contents

PREFACE   9

1   *Background*   11

2   'And a thunder cloud is no name for Papa'   25

3   'One might as well be a jelly fish'   42

4   'Something to do seems coming'   53

5   'How I dread the end of the journey'   68

6   'Papa is the only man I can NOT get on with'   85

7   'Tout passe, tout casse, tout lasse'   111

8   'Their conversation is unrepeatable'   127

9   'I – very much against my will – was married'   135

10 'No other baby will ever be THAT baby'   144

11 *Epilogue*   150

Preface

My mother was born Ellen Peel in August 1863 and died in January 1962, a life span covering more changes in the social scene than in almost any comparable period of history. I was very close to her and though she was forty-five when I was born, it sometimes seemed to me that I lived more in the period of her youth than in my own. When I came to read her letters and diaries they gave me an extraordinary sensation, as if I were the elder, longing to sympathize with and counsel the young Ellen Peel of almost a century ago.

This record, covering a period of just over twenty years of the first half of her life, reaches from 1886, when she started keeping a diary, to 1908, when she married my father and 'lived happily ever after'. Not quite of course, for life is not a fairy tale; there were financial troubles in the early days, there was the trauma of the First World War, with two dearly loved sons at the Front, there was the shattering blow of her husband's death in 1942. She surmounted all these, however, and lived on into a serene old age, surrounded by children, friends and grandchildren. Her great secret was that she was more interested in other people than she was in herself. Instead of turning inwards, as so many old people do, contracting their horizons to their own anxieties and ailments, she always looked outward, eager to hear and to sympathize. I think one of the truest glimpses of her character was given in her obituary in *The Times*: 'If one told her of someone's misfortunes she never said "How sad!" she said immediately: "What can I do to help?".' This characteristic shows itself in these early reminiscences. They give a picture of a vanished world, but through the eyes of a character who is so alive that the gap between then and now seems at times almost infinitesimal.

I

Background

In 1828 Sir Roger Palmer, a respectable if undistinguished Irish baronet, eloped with Mary Ellen Matthews, the daughter of a Welsh solicitor, and took her to Gretna Green. Family tradition says that the bride's father followed close behind in a post-chaise, not to prevent the marriage, but to make sure that the knot was well and truly tied.

It must have been the prevailing Byron-Werther romanticism of the period that made an elopement seem necessary, since in fact the parties were very evenly matched. It is true that, socially, the Palmers were a cut above the Matthewses: they had been granted lands in Ireland in the time of Queen Elizabeth, had acquired a baronetcy in 1777, and were also rather shamefacedly proud of a tenuous connexion with the cuckolded husband of Lady Castlemaine. Miss Matthews's assets, however, were more solid. Her father, the Welsh solicitor, had acquired a considerable fortune, let us hope honestly, and as he had only two daughters and one was childless, the Palmer grandchildren stood to inherit not only their father's Irish estates but the very sizeable Matthews property in North Wales, which was centred on a rather ugly house called Cefn Park on the outskirts of Wrexham. This had originally been a Georgian farmhouse, but later the Palmers in true Victorian taste added two outsize wings containing a dining-room and a billiard-room respectively. There the two little Palmers grew up; Roger, a short, rather undistinguished, good-tempered boy, and Mary Ellen, an altogether more interesting character.

A full-length portrait of Mary Ellen was painted by Sir Francis Grant about 1852. According to the convention of the times she sits on a rock against a background of a lake bordered with trees over which a thunderstorm is shortly about to burst. Her only protection against the elements is a flimsy black lace shawl over an elaborate silk dress with lace ruffles. Unperturbed by the coming catastrophe she gazes out of the picture with large beautiful dark eyes, the faint smile hovering about her full-lipped mouth hardly coming to birth. Although the portrait is full face one can make out the almost flaw-less Grecian profile, straight from the forehead to the end of the nose. Her dark glossy hair is crimped round her face in the then fash-ionable style, her hands are long and supple, the light reflected in the heavy gold and garnet bracelet on her wrist.

Mary Ellen Palmer was beautiful but that was not all. She was spirited, intelligent and extremely well aware of her advantages. Left motherless at an early age, she very much ruled the family roost, and it was almost certainly her influence that induced her father to take her out to the Crimea in 1854 to visit her brother Roger, who was serving in the 23rd Dragoon Guards and had, though she did not know this when she started, taken part in the Charge of the Light Brigade.

She left two diaries of this enterprising trip. One, in copper-plate hand intended obviously for showing around, records their journey to Constantinople and the further excursion to the Crimea itself. There was no attempt on her part to go anywhere near Scutari or the hospitals; Florence Nightingale is never mentioned. Mary Ellen was out to have a good time and she had it. She and her father stayed on board the ship in Balaclava Bay, but Lord Raglan sent down horses for her to ride and she went all over the camp, unper-turbed by the Russian musketry, the freezing cold or the dead horses 'lying about in great abundance', and attended by a bevy of cavaliers.

One of these was Archy Peel, a short red-haired young man with very bright blue eyes, a nephew of the famous Sir Robert. He was not in the Army, but having no profession and nothing particular to do he thought he might as well visit his brothers and friends in the Crimea and take part in a little amateur soldiering. He was nick-named the 'T.G.' or Travelling Gent.

He of course was free, as his rivals were not, to follow the Palmers back to Constantinople when they left the Crimea. He did so and it was soon plain that he was head over heels in love with Mary Ellen. At this point she began to keep a supplementary diary, written on ordinary notepaper in script almost as tiny as that used for the Brontes' *juvenilia*, chronicling the ups and downs of the courtship.

She was much admired in Constantinople, where pretty girls were few and far between, and her diary is full of extracts like the following: 'Ball. Succès. Crowd of introductions. Peel waited patiently to get a dance, it was claimed by three others, everybody striving, admiring looks from strangers. Pink ball dress. Diamond stars in hair. Delightful evening.' Poor 'Peel' was plainly besotted by her. 'He looked at me as if he could eat me,' she wrote, and when she turned cool towards him because at the Opera he seemed to be paying more attention to the stage than to her, he wrote her the wildest and most despairing letter, beginning: 'I am in agony. If loving you to adoration is to wrong you, then I am guilty, then do I deserve the coldness that has wounded me, but not otherwise.'

She was in fact more attracted to him than she liked to acknowledge, but in addition to their emotional tensions both young people suffered from a lack of parental sympathy. It is understandable that the Palmers should not have wished their adored Ellen, a beauty and a very considerable heiress, to marry a younger son with no money and no profession, but it seems odd that the Peels, a completely self-made family, less well born than the Palmers, should also have objected to the match. The Peels, however, had gone into politics which, in those days, held the key to that small, smart, aristocratic circle whose members all knew each other, were mostly related, and were 'in Society'. Moreover they had married upward. Lady Alice Peel, Archy's mother, was a daughter of the Marquess of Ailsa and thought no one quite good enough for herself or her family. Archy had written to her to tell her of his love for Mary Ellen and her reply was chilling. 'Instead of jumping at the match as I thought she would,' Mary Ellen recorded, 'she wrote very coldly if not disapprovingly. Archy was very indignant saying he would be frank at all hazards and send me the letter tho' he knew my pride and delicacy, but he implored me not to abandon him. "My love, my wife you must be or I shall die", he wrote. My pride however revolted at the bare idea of any objection being made to me who am so accustomed to be courted.' It was probably annoyance at the Peel attitude and the accompanying uncertainty that made Mary Ellen so difficult during the next few days. She seems to have quarrelled with Archy on any and every pretext and finally brought the whole matter to a head, putting her point of view with a forcefulness that was certainly unusual in 1855.

We had rather a discussion about the question of a husband's authority over a wife. I told him *plainly* that if I ever married him I could never submit to be dictated to on any subject. I had been accustomed to act independently and I could not give up the habit. *Advice* I could bear but not control and I told him fairly that unless he could promise never to attempt to exercise any authority he must make up his mind to give me up. I made many sacrifices for him and he must make this one for me viz. to abandon his crotchets about a husband's right to control his wife in any case.

Later in the day she asked him

if he had thought of our conversation this morning, he said he had but seemed to be still in the same opinion, he said also that sometimes he felt afraid of me (he meant of marrying me) for if I continued to tease and bully him he might in time not like me. I was nettled at this (for I saw it was a determined struggle on his part for mastery – if he wishes for it now what will it be afterwards) so I said that if it had come to that and he could coolly contemplate the prospect of no longer loving me we had better have nothing more to do with one another. This was said just as we reached home and when we got upstairs the others left the room for a moment and Archy came up to me interrogatively when I repeated what I had said. I never saw a man in such a state as he then was; he took it for a sentence of final separation, said in a hollow voice 'You have intended this for a long time it is only a pretext', walked to the window, stood there for a few moments, gave one great gulping sob, then without listening to me rushed out of the house.

Luckily at this juncture Mary Ellen's brother, Roger, was on leave from the Crimea. He was a quiet unassuming little man, always on the side of peace and kindliness, and his more brilliant sister was very fond of 'Doddy' as she called him. She confided everything to him,

and he listened most kindly, finally advising me to wait a fair time (say a year) to try the strength of my own feelings and then if we both continued the same he promised me his help to bring matters to a happy termination. It was very late when we had done talking but he went afterwards to find Archy and I spent a very uncomfortable night.

Doddy had found Archy sitting under Mary Ellen's bedroom window, though, as she points out 'it was very late and he could not possibly have expected to have been seen', and the next morning the lovesick young man called round to express his penitence.

> He said he had behaved like a brute, called me a noble generous girl for forgiving him and then solemnly promised that I should always do as I liked in everything and that he would give himself to me. It was a solemn abjuration of all his ideas of authority and all his expectations of exerting any control over me should I ever be his wife.

And there alas! the diary ends, on a note of enviable harmony: 'We all went in caïques to the Sweet Waters of Europe, and we were very happy, perfectly reconciled too.'

But it was to take more than the year envisaged by Roger Palmer for Mary Ellen and Archy to sort out their emotional tangles and win over their families. They were not married till 1857 and, at first at any rate, their married life was so stormy that their disapproving relations might well have ventured more than one 'I told you so'. Mary Ellen exacted to the full the promise that she should have her own way in everything. She decided that she and her husband should live, together with her father and brother, on the properties inherited from Grandpapa Matthews. Her children would then become the family heirs and succeed to the very considerable Welsh and Irish estates. (Why she was so sure that Doddy, then quite a young man, would never marry, we can only conjecture.) It was a splendid position for Mary Ellen, with three men at her feet, but for Archy to be the junior and least regarded person in a male trio must have been insufferable. His married life with Ellen was far from smooth. Family tradition has it that there were many violent quarrels, after one of which he slammed out of the house and went to South America. The cause of this *brouille* was said to be the death of his two-year-old son, little Archy, who succumbed to diphtheria after being farmed out to a drainless gardener's cottage while his mother entertained a party for private theatricals at the big house. But this does not seem altogether likely when we read a remarkably bad poem which he wrote to his wife at the time. It is touching in its very ineptitude.

> Though in my boy I lose a son
> God grant I find a wife
> Dearer to me than e'en that one
> This one I love as life.

> That she to me for e'er may prove
> The joy I thirst to find
> O give dear Lord in thy dear Love
> I pray, with all my mind

> That I for her this pilgrimage
> Through Life may soften, Lord
> For Christ his sake, this privilege
> O grant me Mighty Word.

(There are eight more verses but these suffice.)

It seems more probable in view of these lines that the child's death brought about a reconciliation rather than an estrangement between husband and wife. In any case a reconciliation there was. Although all the early victories in their marital life went to Mary Ellen, Archy conquered in the end. He imposed on his wife that relentless pattern of childbirth which overblessed so many Victorian marriages. After little Archy's death there were three more children in quick succession, 1861, 1862, 1863. The last picture of Mary Ellen Peel is a tinted photograph taken during her final pregnancy. She is much changed from the bold lively young woman portray d by Sir Francis Grant. The little curls are gone, her hair is smooth and sleek, drawn back in a heavy chignon. Her face has grown much fuller and is quite expressionless; her hands are folded over a swelling stomach concealed by the full crinoline.

This picture was taken at Brighton, where the Peels had rented a house in Adelaide Crescent, whose semicircle of tall cream painted houses still face the glittering sea. There on August 30th a baby girl was born. A week later, Mr Peel walking in the garden heard a faint cry of 'Archy!', rushed into the house and found his wife dead. When the child was baptized, all that they gave her was her mother's second name. Another Ellen Peel, less beautiful, less selfish, but equally courageous and individual, now took the stage.

Her heartbroken father left England on an extended journey to North and South America and for five years the three little children, Willy, Mary and Ellen, were brought up in their grandfgather's seats, Cefn Park in North Wales, Kenure in county Dublin and the London house in Portland Place. It must have been a strange, rather loveless existence. There was no lady of the house and old Sir Roger was fast sinking into a state of senility. To the end of her life Ellen remembered the long steep stairs of Portland Place, so trying to small legs, and the horror of passing the dust-sheeted drawing-room where some nurserymaid had told them the glimmering white hummocks concealed lions and tigers.

Then in 1868 Archy Peel married again. He chose Lady Georgiana Russell, a daughter of Earl Russell (better known as Lord John). This time there were no family obstacles. The Peels and the Russells, though opposed politically, belonged to the same section of the social world. They were close country neighbours; Pembroke Lodge, the Russells' grace and favour residence at Richmond was, with the aid of the ferry across the River Thames, within twenty minutes of the Peels' Marble Hill at Twickenham. It was obvious that a widower with three young children must marry again, while a lady of twenty-seven would probably, in Victorian days, be only too thankful to find a husband; especially a young lady who did not see eye to eye with her stepmother. Any reader of the *Amberley Papers* or of Bertrand Russell's autobiography will get a very good idea of the cloying atmosphere of Pembroke Lodge. Strains and stresses were as far as possible ignored but they existed. Kate Amberley, Georgiana Russell's sister-in-law, wrote in her diary of 1866: 'I like her (Georgey) so much and think her misunderstood. She never utters a complaint about anyone and there are so many made about her.' And in a letter to Georgiana discussing some family *brouille* she drops the following sentence which speaks volumes: 'The secret (if secret it is) of it all is that Ly. R. is *not* your mother.'

It is remarkable that with this experience behind her Lady Georgiana did not make more of a success of the relationship with her own stepchildren. She had an unrivalled opportunity. They were too young to remember their own mother, they were all affectionate, and Ellen, the youngest, had a heart which positively craved to give and receive love. She used to follow her stepmother around aching to be picked up and petted. Only once did it occur – in church (she supposed afterwards that she had been fidgeting) – and she remembered all her life, though she lived to be ninety-eight, the warmth and softness of that silken bosom. It never, she said, happened again; not a kiss, not a caress. One day, aged about six or seven, she sat down on a garden path and said to herself: 'It's no good. If they won't love me they won't. I shan't try any more.' The wound went deep and was never obliterated.

There was some excuse for Lady Georgiana. She adored her husband and was jealous of all that reminded him of his first wife. The first winter of their marriage the Peels spent at Kenure, lent to Archy by his brother-in-law Roger Palmer. The whole place must have seemed haunted by Mary Ellen. Her full-length portrait hung in the dining-room, presiding at every meal. The small grey church where they worshipped had been built to commemorate her death. Even the bell-pulls still carried the china plaques inscribed: 'Mrs Peel's bedroom', 'Mr Peel's dressing-room'. It was no place to bring a second bride.

They might have remained in Ireland but Georgiana, in her own words, 'could not make up her mind to be cut off from all she had known before' and they returned to England. For Georgiana this was not a very great improvement: they settled in North Wales so that the children (in accordance with Mary Ellen's inheritance plans) should remain near their Palmer relations. The Georgian house that they took, The Gerwyn, was pleasant enough but Denbighshire was difficult of access and a self-centred, unwelcoming county. It was dull for Archy Peel, who had genuine intellectual tastes, but he at least had his hunting. Georgiana did not hunt, she was always having babies or miscarriages, and she did not get on with the neighbours. It must have seemed a long way from Pembroke Lodge and the inner circle of political life.

She made things much worse for herself, too, by raising an implacable opposition in her own home. It was not only her stepdaughters who rebelled against her; her own eldest daughter, Fanny, six years younger than Ellen, made common cause with them. It became an unbridgeable generation gap in which one cannot help feeling that the fault lay with the parents. The young Peels were frequently undutiful, disobedient and disagreeable, but a little love and affection at the outset might have produced a different result.

The sensibilities of young people were not much regarded in those days and nothing was done to promote their self-confidence. The elder Peel girls were always having it rubbed into them that they were plain and unsuccessful. They were not great beauties, it is true, but they were vital, intelligent and amusing, and it will be seen how Ellen, once free of her parents, had no difficulty in making herself popular. At home however the continual snubbing took its toll. Nor were the children helped by the way Lady Georgiana dressed them. Mary Peel remembered with bitterness all her life that she had been made to wear elastic-sided boots at her confirmation and Ellen was taken to dances in her first season wearing a dress bought second-hand from the governess. It was no wonder that they scored very little success in ballrooms. One of their worst trials was being taken to tea with their grandmother Lady Alice at Marble Hill. Lady Alice had been a beauty and had married a rich man for love at the age of nineteen. She catechized her granddaughters about what dances they had been to and what partners they had had. Quite often the answer had to be: 'None at all.' 'Now we know where we are,' Papa said as they came home from their first London dance. 'Very few have danced with you and no one has asked to be introduced to you.'

It seems surprising that under this quenching regime the young Peels were still able to maintain their spirits, but in spite of everything 'cheerfulness kept breaking in'. Once back in the schoolroom they were able to laugh at themselves and at their elders. 'Snubbed at home, ignored abroad' was one of the slogans they coined. Mary, who was an excellent mimic, would take off Lady Ailesbury saying: 'Tea, Duchess? Tea, Lady Georgiana? Tea, Lady So-and-so? Oh' (after a pause and with an abrupt change of voice) 'and you Miss Peel, will you have some tea?' They particularly delighted in the story of what they called 'Ellen's first love affair', which took place at a dinner given by the Melvilles, Lady Georgiana's half-sister and brother-in-law. It was Ellen's first dinner party and she was very young and very shy. There were various minor contretemps: her stepmother signalled to her at dinner that her dress was too low; she tried to hitch up her *décolletage* a little and only succeeded in pulling out a great handful of chemise; which so unnerved her that she left the table still clutching her dinner-napkin. She was however rather consoled when her host, who must have been about sixty, offered to show her some pictures in the back drawing-room and kissed her heartily behind the door. She was so pleased at not being a complete failure that on the way home in the carriage she burst out: 'Wasn't it kind of Uncle William, he kissed me!' There was an inauspicious silence, something had evidently gone wrong. 'He kissed you?' Papa repeated. Even then she did not realize the extent of the catastrophe. 'Yes,' she said, 'when he took me to show me the pictures.' 'And did you kiss him back?' asked Mama. Ellen was an essentially truthful girl and she struggled for exactitude. She thought hard and replied 'I don't remember.' Alas, the exact truth sounded like equivocation and the row that followed was tremendous. Matters were not helped when Uncle William came to call the following Sunday and foolhardily asked Ellen to come down into the hall to help him find his umbrella!

The London seasons, however, played a very small part in the Peel family life, the far greater portion of which was spent at The Gerwyn, about a mile from Bangor-on-Dee and five miles from Wrexham, the local county town. It was a narrow life, both physically and mentally. The Peels were young and active, but they were dependent on their feet or on their horses, which gave them a radius of sixteen miles at most, and on their country neighbours, who were neither very intellectual nor very cultured. Luckily they were provided with two necessary bulwarks against boredom, girl-friends and a useful supply of young men. Like the Miss Bennets of *Pride and Prejudice* they had a regiment quartered nearby, for Wrexham was the depot of the 23rd Regiment, the Welch Fusiliers; and if it was 'absolutely necessary' for the Miss Bennets and the Miss Lucases to 'meet to talk over a ball', the same conditions obtained for the Miss Peels and the Miss Piercys.

The Piercys were a large family who lived at Marchwiel Hall about a mile from The Gerwyn. Their money was newer than the Peels' and in consequence they lived more comfortably, with champagne and ices, a gutta-percha wheeled brougham and an unending supply of chocolates. The three eldest girls, Lily, Florence and Ethel, were near-contemporaries of Mary, Ellen and Fanny Peel and there were few days on which the families did not meet. They had their own vocabulary. 'Affable' was a favourite word of theirs and so was 'cheeky'; casting off a young man was described as 'having a funeral'; if the young man did the casting off the funeral was described as 'compulsory'. Young men were their chief subject of conversation and preeminent among them were the officers of the 23rd with whom they danced and played tennis (backing themselves for bets paid in pairs of gloves), hunted, sketched and flirted. There were endless jokes, teasings and heart-throbs. On one occasion Ellen Peel wrote a parody of a then popular song whose refrain ran:

> It's better than nothing at all;
> Not much!

Each verse was devoted to one of the officers. One of them ran:

> Though his heart he can't spare
> He will give you a stare,
> And that's better than nothing at all,
> Not much!

Lily Piercy illustrated the text with little portraits of the gentlemen in question and there was a tailpiece depicting a gravestone inscribed: 'Here lies the trumpeter of the 23rd. Dead from overwork.' It went all over the county and the Miss Peels were terrified lest their father should see it and guess that they had had a hand in it. For Mr and Lady Georgiana Peel held old-fashioned views even for those days. Mr Peel would not allow his daughters to play rounders, calling it a 'romping game' and comparing it to 'leap-frog and kiss-in-the-ring', an opinion which they rightly considered absurd. Lady Georgiana, when chaperoning a party at the barracks, was 'much perturbed' at not being able to keep them all in the same room. The girls were scolded if they gave the officers a lift, rode home with them from hunting, or even shook hands with them. Naturally the officers knew of all this and it became a regular joke, and perhaps the young ladies behaved worse than they would have done if prohibitions had been more sensible.

'We gave Captain Bertie a lift' wrote Ellen in her diary 'for which, as he remarked, "we should both catch it if known".' This diary, which she kept very fully for the years 1886, 1887 and 1888, gives an authentic, though at times a surprising account of ordinary country house life in the second half of the nineteenth century. Its interest lies partly in the fact that it connects two widely disparate periods, and partly in the unflinching candour of the writer. Victorian ladies were supposed to express their personal opinions decorously and, if need be, hypocritically. Not so Ellen Peel, 'Papa and Mama were quite superlatively nasty,' she writes, or 'Papa announced his intention of going to Rhyl. Everybody (of us) delighted, for he has really been too cross.' Her verdict on Mama after a quarrel was: 'She must be cracked', and, on another occasion: 'I had strong leanings towards step-matricide.' Nor does she spare herself. She faithfully records the unpleasant things the neighbourhood says about her and her sisters; that they run after the officers, that someone says she and Mary are the plainest girls they have ever seen, that she talks too much, that she snubs people. 'Will no-one ever say anything nice about me?' she queries rather pathetically.

The diary is limited in scope. *Punch* at the beginning of 1887 decorated the front page of its almanack with a little frieze of drawings illustrating the events that might be anticipated in the coming year. They show the Jubilee celebrations, the opening of the Imperial Institute, Gladstone in bed with a drunken Irishman dancing on his stomach and brandishing a bottle of Home Rule, a lady in a steeple hat advocating Welsh Home Rule, Father Thames forced to swallow a dose of purification, and a Girton girl in mortar board and pince-nez apparently admonishing a football Blue. No echo of all this seems to have found its way into North Wales. The drawings inside the almanack however, which accompany the somewhat feeble *Punch* jokes, give a very good idea of what Ellen Peel and her sisters looked like and what they were doing. There are young ladies out hunting, riding side-saddle, their long trailing skirts covering the tips of their boots, their tight-fitting habits clipped in at the waist, emphasizing their swelling bosoms. There are young ladies playing tennis on rather rough lawns with squarish oblong racquets, wearing skirts down to the ground with enormous protuberances behind, their heads crowned by strange little conical hats with round brims. And there are young ladies in flowing voluminous afternoon dresses and Princess of Wales fringes, telling fortunes by means of palmistry over the tea-table in a comfortable crowded Victorian drawing-room, (Ellen was rather good at this but naturally Papa disapproved. He said 'it was just an excuse for holding young men's hands.')

All these diversions are recorded in Ellen Peel's diary, which transports us to another world, now lost for ever. It is a world of tennis parties, mixed cricket matches, hunting, private theatricals, decorating the church, visiting the poor, flirting with the officers. In short the world of Jane Austen and of Trollope.

Amid the uncertainties, the hurry and the ugliness of today, this world may seem to glow with a certain nostalgic charm, but reading the diary one realizes that the superficially pleasant existence it chronicles was vitiated by two things. One was the triviality of the life, which among other drawbacks catered for no intellectual interests. Ellen was unusually intelligent, but the Peel girls were under-educated. Indifferent governesses had drummed French and German into them, Papa did his best by summoning them every morning into his dressing-room to read them Bishop Berkeley and Locke's *Essay Concerning Understanding*, and there was a certain amount of desultory reading; but there was no stimulating conversation, no flow of ideas to be found either at home or in the county. Ellen may not have been conscious of this vacuum, but what she was aware of was the purposelessness of her existence. She records at the beginning of 1887 a talk she had with her eldest half-brother, Teddy. 'He was thinking how one would feel when dying if one had never done anything but amuse oneself. He is about right. But what is one to do in the present circumstances? It is so different for a man.' How many Victorian young ladies must have echoed the last seven words!

Another cause for unhappiness was of course the unpleasant home atmosphere. This sometimes went as far as blows. 'We went to the cookery class in the afternoon,' Ellen wrote. 'It was rather fun. Mama boxed my ears before starting which somewhat surprised me and I complained to Papa who also seemed astonished. We had a very cheerful cookery lesson.' And again, six months later: 'I had a fight with Mama, she fell on me, and then complained I hurt her! But I am thoroughly ashamed of having let her fight with me.' But Mama's blows were nothing like so hurtful as Papa's wounding tongue. His unkindness was made so much worse because Ellen, who never cared for her stepmother, was basically devoted to her father. His jibes must have been very hard to forgive. Once, when he was taking her to the Naval Review at Portsmouth, he thought fit to tell her that she had got herself up like a 'Merry Andrew'. Once, out hunting, that she 'looked like a sack cut in two with a string'. 'Papa said I was a spectacle!' Ellen wrote, 'and everybody laughed at me out hunting and he was ashamed.' Even at this distance in time one finds it hard to forgive Papa.

2

'And a thunder cloud is no name for Papa'

In 1886, when Ellen's diaries begin, the Peel family consisted of: Papa and Mama; Mary and Ellen, who were exactly a year apart and were, at this date, twenty-four and twenty-three respectively; Willy, their glamorous elder brother, now serving with the Army in Egypt; and seven half-brothers and sisters. Fanny, the eldest of these, who had just come out, was followed by Teddy, at Eton, three younger brothers at various schools, and two little girls being educated, more or less, by an Alsatian governess, Mlle Schlenker. At Cefn Park, about two miles from The Gerwyn, lived Sir Roger and Lady Palmer. As we have seen, Mary Ellen's plan had been for her brother to remain unmarried and make her children his heirs. He appears to have fallen in with this meekly enough, but Mary Ellen died and her eldest child and only son proved wildly extravagant. After twice settling his nephew's debts, Sir Roger, who had now succeeded to the baronetcy, decided to marry and beget an heir of his own. He chose a Miss Roper, a girl only eight years older than his nieces, who dutifully called her 'Aunt Milly'. It was another carefully designed plan that ended in disappointment. Sir Roger remained childless.

This was the family set-up. It was a restricted and rather dull environment, but the younger generation found a certain amount of excitement and enlivenment in the presence of the officers of the Fusiliers. The ones who chiefly figure in the diary are: Colonel Brown, who commanded the regiment; Captain Bertie, also known as 'the Hon. B.' since he was a younger son of the Earl of Abingdon; Captain Fenwick, who made eyes indiscriminately, but rather more at Mary Peel; Mr Engleheart, or 'the Angel'; and Mr Cooper, by whom Fanny was rather attracted. In addition to these there was 'Sav', Major-General Sir Savage Mostyn, KCB, who was retired but still seemed to feel himself a part of his old regiment. Although he was fifty-one he was conducting a violent flirtation with Mary Peel aged twenty-four, and the ups and downs of this affair caused Ellen many anxious moments. Her own principal young man was Captain Bertie, though more on a ragging than a flirtatious basis.

In addition to the officers there were the country neighbours. First and foremost came the Piercys, an unfailing stand-by. Then came Captain and Mrs Cowan, who were not approved of by Lady Georgiana, who said they allowed their house to become a meeting-place for the girls and the officers. Ellen however was very fond of them, particularly of Captain Cowan ('*The*' Captain as she affectionately called him, to distinguish him from the whipper-snappers of the 23rd). There were also the grander county families – the Wynns, the Cholmondeleys and the Hill-Trevors – and there were lesser fry, Mr McGonigle, the vicar of Bangor-on-Dee, whom Ellen described as 'dinnery', and Muff and Connie Edwards, the daughters of another clerical family, and their brother, who bore the unattractive nickname of 'Sneezer'. (Nicknames were current, though presumably not in the presence of their bearers, but it is curious that the Christian names of the opposite sex were never used. One might read every word of the diary without discovering that Captain Fenwick was baptized George and Captain Bertie Reginald, though they are mentioned on nearly every page.)

A recent addition to Denbighshire society was Mrs Talbot, a sprightly widow, who had taken a house at Ellesmere in Shropshire. Mrs Talbot, known as 'Tabby' or 'Tabby the Cat', must have been at least ten years older than the Peel girls (she had married in 1874) but this did not prevent her making a determined and at times successful set at Mary Peel's two admirers, Sav and Captain Fenwick. Although she was consumptive she was extremely vivacious. ' "If she has only one lung," said Colonel Brown, "what does anyone want with more?" '; and Ellen describes her on one occasion as being 'very much on the laugh'. Needless to say, both Mary and Ellen Peel cordially disliked her.

But now let us come to the diary itself. It begins on a hot summer's day at the end of August 1886, and immediately we are back in a more leisurely world.

Sunday August 29th

Very hot. We went to Bangor church and Mr McGonigle preached. Papa and Mama came for second service and we all

stayed. Mr Cooper and Mr Engleheart walked over in the afternoon and the whole family sat in a solemn circle on the lawn,
but things improved after tea and we clipped the dogs and picked
nuts and then walked part of the way back with them, not far,
by Mama's especial desire.

Monday August 30th

Mary's and my birthday. How I hate getting so old. Colonel
Brown and Captain Bertie came in the afternoon. He is going to
give me a copy of Watts' hymns. [This was a tease. Ellen was
quick-tempered and some allusion to 'let dogs delight' is probably
intended.] Great harmony prevailed at dinner till Mama said she
had invited a few people on Wednesday which fell like a bomb-
shell on Papa.

Tuesday August 31st

Workhouse treat. Papa still so cross he refused to receive them.
It passed off as usual. We fiddled and Lily Piercy sang etc. [It
shows the prevalence of amateur music in Victorian days and its
very low standard. Lily Piercy had rather a pretty voice but Mary
and Ellen Peel were quite unmusical and practically tone deaf.
Nevertheless they played the violin and 'cello respectively.] Mama
was so tired she went to bed in hysterics and a thunder cloud
is no name for Papa.

Wednesday September 1st

Papa went off to shoot at Cefn. Mama had a bad headache,
but she really behaved beautifully which none of us expected.
Col. Brown, Capt. Bertie, Mr Engleheart, Mr Cooper, Charlie Hill-
Trevor and the Piercys came for lawn tennis. We had a few good
sets. Capt. Bertie interfered with ours, he wanted me to play with
him. Mary had her hands free as Sav departed after the adieu in
the conservatory maliciously interrupted by Capt. Bertie. Things
blacker still in the evening.

Thursday September 2nd

Papa announced his intention of going to Rhyl. Everybody (of
us) delighted except Fanny who has got to go too, for he has really
been too cross.

Saturday September 4th

Ladies' cricket match at Marchwiel Hall. Mrs Darby brought over the Oswestry crew. I think, take them all round, they were the ugliest lot I ever saw. However they made 156. Ethel [Piercy] bowled very well, but an infant fiend would block everything. I kept wicket and caught two. Of our side only Lady Cholmondeley made a score, 32 not out, Ethel was bowled for 7, Miss Ethelstan run out and I caught for 6, a bee stung me.

Tuesday September 7th

Mary and I drove to Mrs Ormrod's at Pen-y-lan. Capt. Bertie was great fun at tea with the cakes. I played with him in the last set and shied a bun at him. I wish I hadn't. I always mean to be quiet and always forget. We sat on the same bench and tucked the rug round us and again I wished I hadn't. Alas Tabby has returned. We really do not want her.

Friday September 10th

Cricket match. The afternoon was dull, but later on, who should appear but Tabby! After the most affectionate greetings she took my place in a set, but I forgave her, for later on Sav appeared and she of course made a set at him, but I am happy to add was totally outgeneralled by Mary. He, for once, behaved quite unexceptionally. I devoted myself to the Angel, who was sick and sorry but most amiable, and administered a B. and S. which made him worse.

Saturday September 11th

Papa, Mama and Fanny went to a party at the barracks. As I had failed to secure a pressing invitation for three, I stayed away, in hopes my absence would cause a sensation, but I regret to add it did not, as nobody even asked after me but our invariable friend Col. Hutton and Capt. Bertie. Mary went to see Capt. Bertie's rooms under proper chaperonage, and they had all the best sets and enjoyed themselves, but they had to go very early, because of Papa's cough, and, as usual, nothing came of it. [This presumably means that there was no forward move from Sav.] I umpired, with great dignity, at a match between the Bangor boys and Fergus' team which won. [Fergus was a younger half-brother, then aged nine.] They were evidently unaccustomed to umpiring as they questioned all my decisions, refused to go out, counted the overs themselves and objected to the scoring. However they were overruled. Summer is over and I deeply regret it.

Tuesday September 14th

We went to the [tennis] club and had some very good sets, the Angel and Mary against Col. Hutton and me, which I lost 2s. on, and Col. Hutton and me against Col. Graham and Mary, which she lost 4s. on. Capt. Bertie came in later in his shooting clothes and we gave him a lift for which, as he remarked, we should catch it if known. He and the Angel were both fascinating. Tabby was there as usual arranging a breakfast party, but we did her. The preternatural good humour of the family has broken up, chiefly owing to our 'indepence'.

Friday September 17th

Cricket match at the Piercys between Civil and Military. They went in first. Mr Engleheart stayed in all the time and made over 60. They agreed to play it out, and we just won, the finish was most exciting. I won 2s. from Col. Brown and one from the Angel, who was snubbed by him for paying it in public. Lily seriously owns to being gone on him and I really think it is true.

Monday September 20th

We went to the Griffiths' in the afternoon. Mrs Griffiths had a good tea and an excellent idea of making one comfortable. The excitement now is our match against Gen. Mostyn and Capt. Bertie. I betted a pair of gloves with the Angel, 'not old ones', as he said. Lily still much gone.

Tuesday September 21st

We went to luncheon with Tabby, found Col. Brown, Capt. Fenwick and Gen. Mostyn there. Capt. Fenwick looks all right again and made eyes at us all, especially Mary. His star was quite in the ascendant today, he had his buttonhole pinned in, ate the peaches, walked through the wood etc. The General was nowhere. We went to the Club afterwards, found the Angel, Capt. Griffiths, Charlie Hill-Trevor and Capt. Bertie there. I first played a single with him and then they insisted on our playing the match, and with umpires, scorers etc. ad. lib. we began, very much against my will. The others took chairs round, and with great solemnity, owing to the bets, we started, but, when at 3-2, so many spectators arrived that we stopped. Capt. Bertie wanted

very much to go on and we finally persuaded him to split up and
he and I played the others. Afterwards we played with Charlie
Trevor and Capt. Fenwick and of course the General, much
against my will as I wanted the Angel or Capt. Bertie. Sav was
not a bit amiable, but Capt. Fenwick made up for him, 'cheeky
fellow', as Mary said on the way back. Nobody paid much attention to Tabby. She was rather more amiable than usual.

Wednesday September 22nd
    The neighbourhood, amiable as usual, says Mary and I run
after the General and Capt. Bertie. Mrs Griffiths has heard that
Fanny was the nicest of the three. Cheek!

Ellen had perhaps been previous in announcing that summer was
over on September 14th since the tennis parties and cricket matches
continued, but towards the end of the month autumn and its principal diversion fairly set in, for the hunting season began. Archy Peel
was one of the best riders to hounds in England. The local hunt, the
Wynnstay, was inclined to regard him rather sourly, for he rode
better and harder than any other member of it, and won the Hunt
Steeplechase with monotonous regularity. His daughters, however,
admired him tremendously, followed him, with little regard for
their own necks, as closely as they could, and were inclined to des-
pise more timid riders. 'Went out in the afternoon.' Ellen recorded
on one occasion, 'Papa and his 5 daughters' (the youngest was aged
eight), 'found the hounds but *not* the field.' Out riding they had to
keep their horses' heads in a strict military line, not one inch forward or back; and they were never allowed to let a horse refuse.
(They once spent two-and-a-half hours trying to get a horse over
some obstacle and finally had to send for Papa, who popped it over
at the first try!) Nor were they allowed to go into the stables to pet
or enquire after their horses, though this prohibition may not have
been ase unreasonable as it sounds, for Archy Peel, in advance of his
time, used to employ discharged prisoners in an effort to reform
them.* It must, on the other hand, have been pure contrariness that

---

* One's heart slightly warms to the tiresome but courageous old man when one
hears that on one occasion, returning home with his daughter in the dog-cart, he
was met by a flustered head groom relating that one of the ex-gaolbirds was in
the yard with a gun, 'swearing to get Mr Peel'. The latter bade Ellen get down and
drove in under the archway at a walk. 'No man,' he said, 'is going to keep me out
of my own stable-yard.'

made him refuse to tell his daughters till the night before the meet what horses they were to ride or even if they were going out at all. Nevertheless the hunting field gave the girls quite a few chances of evading parental discipline and of indulging in tête-à-têtes with the opposite sex, of which Papa would certainly not have approved.

Friday September 24th

Hounds met at the Hopyard. We had great fun. Capt. Fenwick was in great form all round, we chaffed him about Tabby. Capt. Bertie and I discussed the old question, men and women, who was badly treated, marriage etc. The General was much taken up with his horse, and not satisfactory except for one brief interval.

Sunday September 26th

Bangor Church. We all stayed for the Holy Communion. In the afternoon General Mostyn and Capt. Fenwick come over from Erbistock [General Mostyn's house]. The General behaved rather better. We walked part of the way back with them. Capt. Fenwick offered me a lead out hunting. It was rather fun, but Papa said mildly but firmly, that it 'must not happen again'.

Monday October 4th

Mary could not come out as Overall was lame. The hounds met at Erddy's and the rest of us went. Capt. Cowan, Capt. Bertie, the Angel, Capt. Fenwick. Mr Cooper, Tabby etc. were out. I quarrelled with Capt. Bertie about the tobogganing but afterwards made it up and rode with him all the time nearly. We lost the hounds and rode ever so far together, talked about our ideals etc. He was rather nice and very amusing but soon went home. Afterwards I rode with Capt. Fenwick. He was making eyes as usual, but instead of going any further, told me he was thinking of getting married to a widow with £3,000 a year. I wished him joy and everything and we shook hands on it. I was intensely disgusted but nearly roared with laughter thinking as we always had of him as the Refuge. [Presumably a refuge from spinsterhood, though why they should have regarded Captain Fenwick with his flirtatious propensities in that light is not quite clear. Perhaps they thought him so susceptible that any determined effort could secure him – unlike the wily Sav.]

Saturday October 8th

We drove to the Trotting Mare and got on. We stayed in the woods nearly all day, had one little gallop and risked out necks many times. I rode so far with Capt. Fenwick and talked about love, marriage, trying to be good, women and such subjects. He is rather nice, but I don't believe one ought to talk so much of such things. Conversation as I had with Dr Lloyd, about getting down one's weight is much more sensible. [Doctor Lloyd was a hard-riding medical practitioner, something of a figure in the Wynn-stay Hunt. He once offered to mount any of the girls 'because he knew that none of Mr Peel's daughters would ride crooked'. This was a credit to Papa's rigorous training because in the days when all ladies rode side-saddle they were inclined to lean over too far to the pommel side and the badly distributed weight gave their horses sore backs.] I missed Papa and Fanny and rode home with the Cowans across country. Papa was rather angry and Mama furious when I got back. Mr Howard advised me to say I was with the hounds, but Mama [with unwonted sarcasm] said 'I should go back and tell Papa the best way to get to the fox.'

North Wales was certainly not the liveliest of environments. It had its compensations for a healthy young woman fond of games and hunting but its intellectual stimulus was non-existent. It had not always been so. When the Peels first settled at The Gerwyn there had been entertaining visitors. One of the earliest had been Woolner, the Pre-Raphaelite sculptor, who had been a college friend of Archy Peel's and who had been commissioned to design a memorial to the latter's first wife. He chose to depict her standing with clasped hands watching an angel bearing away her baby, who had died of typhoid, it will be remembered, after being farmed out in an undrained cottage. It is rather a beautiful work, carried out in white marble and showing Ellen Peel's Greek profile. It stands in the parish church at Wrexham, but the bronze casting from which the marble was copied remained in the hall at The Gerwyn. One wonders if Lady Georgiana really appreciated it!

Other visitors to The Gerwyn in those early days included Tennyson, who came to stay more than once. He read 'The Northern Farmer' aloud to the family in such a thick Lincolnshire accent they could scarcely make out a word, and he further compromised his popularity by lifting Mary Peel onto his knee. She was seventeen and much resented being treated as a little girl, but the poet only boomed in his deep voice: 'Many young ladies would be proud to sit on my knee!' This was true; Margot Tennant at about the same period was honoured by such an invitation, but the Peel girls thought it insufferably conceited and much preferred Robert Browning, who attended the local race meeting looking not at all like a poet but like a jolly gentleman farmer, in a suit of checks that the critical young ladies considered far too loud.

By 1886 however all these interesting contacts had vanished. Almost the only visitors who came to stay at The Gerwyn during the three years recorded in the diary were Mama's sister-in-law, Lady Ribblesdale, and her daughter Ady. Ellen, who was not disposed to admire her stepmother's relations, described Aunt Emma as 'sighing more than ever', and Ady as 'heavy-lively'. 'On such subjects as the kitchen range and her mother's shawl, she grows quite animated.' To entertain these not very stimulating guests the Peels gave a dinner party.

Tuesday October 5th

Fanny arranged the flowers and I painted some menus. Capt. Fenwick, the Angel, Sneezer and Mr McGonigle came to dinner. They were fearfully and wonderfully dull, a dead silence was generally imminent, I sat between the Angel and Sneezer. They had Ady Lister and Mama on their other sides, so both wanted to talk to me, but I was so awfully heavy that they both succumbed. The Angel informed me I was always talking and he hated chatterboxes. Sneezer let out about the paper chase. I thought Mama knew. The parrot [*i.e.* Capt. Fenwick] was deadly dull. He pumped Mary to find out if I had told her [about his intended proposal to the widow with £3,000 a year], he deeply regrets having told me. The others thought he was making up to me, I knew better (now), but have to take the credit for it. Afterwards we played games; 'I filled my ship', hiding things in conspicuous places, riddles, etc. The Angel was preternaturally sharp and everyone else proportionately dull. Papa was gloomy. After they were gone he sent for us and in fear we went. He first informed us that on no account were we to disgrace ourselves by running in the paper chase. Then that Willy was on the point of being posted as a defaulter at Newmarket. I *cannot* understand it. Papa is much shocked, but I cannot see that it is morally worse than before though of course more disagreeable. But then it is a three-cornered world. The only thing that I am clear about is that it is our place to pay up.

This is the first time that Willy Peel has been mentioned in his sister's diary, except for a note at the very beginning saying that he had gone back to Egypt where he was on Kitchener's staff. 'He has a Major's pay,' wrote Ellen, 'but Uncle Roger has stopped his allowance, he expects to be away for two years and we shall miss him horribly.' Papa and Uncle Roger took a very different view. They regarded Willy, if not precisely as a thorn in the flesh, as an intractable problem and were only too pleased to have him out of the country.

William Frederick seemed at first to have been born under a lucky star. He was unusually good-looking, full of charm and gaiety, and supposed to be heir to his rich uncle. Even his stepmother, so unloving to his sisters, had, at any rate to start with, a soft spot for the engaging little boy. Thomas Woolner writing to Archy Peel sent a special message to 'my darling little friend Will-Fred'. He was popular wherever he went and his sisters, particularly Ellen, adored him.

Willy was originally destined for the Navy and was especially picked as one of the midshipmen to sail in the *Bacchante* with the Duke of Clarence and the future George V. After the voyage he unfortunately gambled at Malta so heavily that, quite literally, in addition to everything else he lost all his shirts. He was shipped home and accommodated with a commission in the 2nd Life Guards. He took to smart London life like a duck to water and was soon moving in the Marlborough House set. He stayed at Sandringham and entranced his provincial sisters with accounts of the Princess of Wales turning somersaults over the backs of the sofas, with her long skirts so beautifully tucked in that one never caught the smallest glimpse of an ankle. Ellen was amused by the way the Prince used to ask the young officers of the Household Brigade to Marlborough House to gamble and then send them Christmas cards adjuring them to lay off it. It would have been a good thing if Willy could have followed the advice rather than the example. He was hopeless about money and continually in debt. It was this that drove his father and Uncle Roger to the verge of desperation.

The diary will soon focus very much more on Willy, but in the meantime the somewhat trivial round of life in North Wales went on much as usual.

Sunday October 10th

Had a real row at breakfast about the marmalade, and another afterwards about the dance. Mama got it up, she is abominably cheeky, and Papa tried to impress us and failed. Sav came over in the afternoon. He is very anxious for Mary to come out hunting. I regret to say he made love to her again. They ought to be engaged. Papa says he is too old and does not care for her, but if I knew as little as he does I should hold my tongue.

Monday October 11th

Had a long letter from Willy. He has been made Head of the Intelligence Department, besides being an ADC to General Kitchener and Major in the Egyptian Army. He is getting on very well. It is all moonshine about his being posted, as matters are just where they were.

Tuesday October 12th

Mrs Lee's dance, nominally from 8–12. We got there late. Most of our set were not there. Tabby was there, the Edwards[es], the Piercys in mauve looked very nice, in fact we all took rather a back seat to them. There were lots of pretty people there. The ladies were a dream, but the men a nightmare, a nondescript lot, with unbrushed hair and remarkable clothes. Capt. Fenwick sat out with me. He told me he had been down to Derbyshire, been refused and thrown up the sponge. He behaved awfully well about it, but he should not squeeze one's hand directly after. The great excitement was watching Lily and Muff [Edwards] contest for the Angel. Lily won, 6–5, but she dances best. Fanny wore white, Mary and I grey and roses.

Wednesday October 13th

Meet at Sarn. It rained most of the time and we sheltered and then rode home in couples, Fanny and Mr Cooper, Mary and Fenwick, Sneezer and I. Mary was *au mieux* with Fencock. I don't

feel it my duty so much to warn her now. He said he did not remember our conversation last night and then asked me why I
blushed, as if there were anything to blush about. Fanny got
dropped onto in the afternoon. Papa threatened to put up all our
banns, said they had long noticed Mr Cooper's attentions to her,
that girls should not ride with penniless young men, that the book
of a girl's mind should not be turned over and thumbed – except
by anyone who has money. That was the English of it. That
Mary had fixed her affections (not on things above, like Lily) that
he could not marry her, that her young life would be blighted
and she might now be an old maid!

Friday October 15th

Meet at Penley. I rode all the morning with Capt. Fenwick.
who said he felt 'desperate'. I expect he is feeling pretty bad, for
he had made pretty sure of it. We missed Papa. Capt. Fenwick
rode home with us. He told us our faults, we told him his. He is
about the greatest flirt I know but very nice. Mama and Mary
think he means to propose to one of us. I know better, but can't
well tell them.

Saturday October 16th

Mary and I went over to the Piercys in the afternoon. Florence
drew a capital caricature of the Angel, and we stuck on an aureole
and a pair of wings. He was dancing with Muff, and though
we tore off the head Mr Cooper recognized it. Lily was made very
unhappy by hearing that the Angel had lunched at the Vicarage
[the Edwardses' home] on his way up. To watch Mary and Lily is
enough to make one swear never to have a penchant. Sav and
Mary sat side by side and of course everything happened as usual.
He told me to take care of her last thing. He is really coming on,
learning to make pretty speeches. Capt. Bertie is back, Sav says
with a smile he is 'distrait'. Fanny was scowled at at dinner and
pitched into in the evening (chiefly about Mr Cooper) besides not
having the fun. I call it a great shame and very bad for her to
have such ideas put into her head.

Sunday October 17th

Rained, so we had prayers at home. Papa was talking about the
Eucharist, he thinks Christ meant the Church by His Body.

Wednesday October 20th

Papa took Fanny out in the Clifden in the afternoon. They had a smash in the Red Lane. Sprite whipped round, the carriage got in the ditch, Papa was thrown out, the wheel passed over him and the harness all kicked to pieces, but luckily no harm was done, no one hurt.

Thursday October 21st

Mary and I went over to the Piercys. Lily had been to stay with the Cat, and was chockful of news. She says the General has proposed to her twice. If he has, he has behaved like a real cad. She also says it would not be honourable to tell whether Capt. Fenwick did or not (where is the difference?) and that Major Stewart did several times. She never made Lily promise not to repeat it and I believe it was coined for the occasion. She says Capt. Bertie laughs at me. She also said some most unrepeatable things, which no nice, almost no respectable woman would say. It would seem a shame to repeat what she said only as she does not mind telling her love affairs, why should anybody else? She hardly knows Lily. Mary was unhappy. I think it is rather a good thing, as she ought either to be engaged to the General or quite break with him, whether it is true or not.

Friday October 22nd

Went to ask after Parker the mole-catcher. He is no better.

Saturday October 23rd

Papa and I drove to Gane's Wood. We are late for the meet but picked them up directly. Gen. Mostyn was out. I was to ask him over on Sunday, as Mary means to put an end to it. After much trouble I cornered him and he promised to come, but I felt rather like a traitor. Capt. Fenwick was out, he informed me that he had heard I was going to be married. I knew who to, but of course pretended not. I told him what Mrs Talbot had said. He asked me so confidently whether she had said he had proposed that I could not resist. Capt. Bertie was out. I reproached him for laughing at me, but he only laughed a great deal more and made me laugh and rode after me when I rode away. He has heard the report, which is very tiresome he said, feeling by that that no one might speak to anyone without it being said they were engaged.

Papa was affable on the way back, but got sentimental on duty when near home.

Sunday October 24th

Papa came down in a beastly temper, so of course Mama followed suit. We went to Bangor church. We expected Gen. Mostyn and Capt. Fenwick. Mary meant to pitch into him and bring things to an end, but luckily for himself he never came.

Monday October 25th

Gen. Mostyn and Capt. Fenwick called here. They met the children [Ethel aged twelve, Grace aged ten], who told them Papa was coming, when, as Ethel said in the evening, 'Capt. Fenwick said "By Jove" and Gen. Mostyn walked away so quick that he could scarcely keep up with him.' Papa looks on them as he says 'as our future sons and brothers-in law'. They all expect us to marry them. Papa says it will be very bad behaviour on one side or the other if we don't. Even Mary seems to expect it. No one understands my hints and no one knows except myself. If Mary breaks off with Gen. Mostyn and something don't turn up, we shall feel infinitesimally small. What ought I to do if they *will* flirt, knowing what I know under a sacred promise? By the by they asked for us, but luckily for us, the parlourmaid did not say so.

Monday November 1st

Papa and I went to Odford Racecourse. The meet was not advertised, so there were not many people out. They found at Royalty and had a short gallop from there, and then at Mr Whitmore's cover where they found again, and had a very nice gallop. I followed Papa, and there was no one in front but him and Lady Cholmondeley. Foxhall jumped beautifully. I hit the branch of a tree very hard, knocked off the outside of my hat but kept the lining. I got into a ditch and scratched my face. I rode with Capt. Bertie a good deal, but I think he is rather shy of me since the report. I asked Abyse about the Ladies' uniform, and then wished I hadn't, as the button has been given to some and we are not among them.

'Abyse' was the daughter of Sir Watkin Williams-Wynn, MFH. The Wynns were the great people of North Wales and Sir Watkin succeeded Sir Watkin at Wynnstay as Louis succeeded Louis on the throne of France. The Wynnstay Hunt was originally known as Sir Watkin Williams-Wynn's Hounds and was (and still is) frequently alluded to as 'Sir Watkin's'. The uniform refers to the button and the collar which Masters of Hounds bestow on supporters of the Hunt. In the 'eighties the custom arose of allowing their female relations to sport the insignia. It was not given to the Peels on the rather lame pretext that Mr Peel did not actually own any covers. The truth is that the Peels were not popular in North Wales. Papa alleged that this was so because Lady Georgiana, a newcomer to the county, took precedence, as an Earl's daughter, over all the local wives; but it may have been because of his own abrasive personality and it certainly owed something to his hard riding. He was always in front with the hounds and lesser men resented it, accusing him of steeplechasing instead of hunting. His daughters probably made things no better by their own rather scornful attitude towards the rear of the field. 'We met most of the people coming back,' Ellen wrote on one occasion, 'after a good run. A ladies' run, I think, they were all so enthusiastic about it.'

Wednesday November 3rd

Opening meet at Bryn-y-pys. The new uniforms came out. They have not offered us the button which is cheek. However one comfort is that the buff [the colour of the Wynnstay Hunt collar] makes them look sallower than usual. Ethel [her younger sister] was under my care, so I rode with her nearly all day. Rode with Capt. Bertie a good deal but not so much as I used. Miss Ethel professed herself as extremely sorry 'to spoil sport'. It poured all day and there was no run. We *insisted* on Mary's performing her duty, so she rode home with him [General Mostyn], and much against her will took him to task. He quite denied it [proposing to Mrs Talbot], and laughed at the idea. What a liar that woman must be. However she [Mary] did not do what we told her, but went on flirting and neither brought it on nor broke it off. She really is in love with him which upsets one's calculations. I wonder what it feels like. Why don't I fall in love? It is quite time, nearly all my female friends have been crossed in love and why aren't I? They all go about confiding their secrets and I am quite out of it with nothing to confide.

Thursday November 4th

Papa wrote two very good letters about the roads in the *Morning Post*, got an answer from 'Cyclist' and smashed him. We went to tea with Mrs Cowan. She lectured us on our faults, sharp way of answering, snubbing, etc. Fanny tea'd with Ethel [Cowan] who imparted to her, in the strictest confidence, that that cat Abyse Wynn said of me yesterday: 'Now that Capt. Bertie, Cooper & Co. are gone, Ellen Peel hooks on to that miserable Charlie Hill-Trevor.' I felt as much surprised as did the prophet Balaam on a similar occasion. Nothing like experience, I can quite picture his feelings. Also that Mrs Cowan herself thinks me one of the plainest girls she ever saw, but the Captain stands up for us both. Will anybody ever say anything nice about me, I wonder?

When we came in there were some nice long letters from Willy. What a dear he is. He has had a touch of fever and has been under fire, seems to be enjoying himself. I suppose it is good for him being out there but one misses him here dreadfully.

Monday November 8th

Went to see Parker the mole-catcher. He was not quite so well today.

Friday November 12th

Meet at Broughten. They found at Lasses and ran to Grafton 36 mins with only one check. Mary had a fall and got hung up by her stirrup but Overall stood still till she was picked up. Connie Lovett had two falls and was dragged – rather hurt. Sir Watkin swore in general and at Papa in particular. Fanny and I followed Papa, we were well up, there were only very few at the first check. As Dr Lloyd said, it was heavenly. After Grafton they ran by the Scair and killed in Malpas churchyard, but I came down at a wire fence and stood on my head in the water for some time. I had to go home after that as I was all wet and full of mud, nearly drowned as someone said. Capt. Fenwick and Fanny caught me up near Bangor, and he made eyes even then, which was an effort of self sacrifice I have rarely seen equalled.

Friday November 26th

Hounds met at Crosslanes. I rode with Capt. Bertie and Capt. Fenwick nearly all day. Capt. Bertie talked a great deal about being in love, men and women etc., when they are hard hit he thinks men stick to it. Capt. Fenwick did nothing in particular, beyond particularly wanting to shake hands, but the brute says Fanny goes the best. Mrs Talbot was out, but rather out of it. Sav rode a good deal with Mary and was middling.

Saturday December 11th

Meet at Hollybush Gate. Coming home Capt. Fenwick asked Mary to ride back with him, when Capt. Bertie whipped him off in front, leaving us to follow to our great indignation – it looked so bad, and Papa saw, as we heard next day. I had a funeral directly I got home.

If a young man offended, among the Peels and the Piercys, you did not speak to him or acknowledge his existence until he was forgiven and 'the corpse' was 'resurrected'. Captain Bertie's resurrection this time did not take place till Christmas Eve. Meanwhile there was a hard frost and ice hockey took the place of hunting. The younger boys came back from school and Mama, who had been on a visit to her ducal relations, returned 'quite abominably cheeky after Woburn'. There was the usual bustle over presents and Christmas cards and church decorations (the Miss Peels were responsible for the font, which they did in holly and cottonwool). The year however ended on a sour note. 'I was very angry with Papa', wrote Ellen on December 30th, 'who said I was the vulgarest person he had ever seen, and could not get over it all day.'

3

'One might as well be a jelly fish'

In many ways 1887 was almost a carbon copy of 1886. The days were still occupied by hunting and ice hockey in the winter, tennis and cricket in the summer. There were dances and private theatricals to afford scope for gossip. The flirtations underwent some slight rearrangements: Lily Piercy gave up the Angel and embarked on a more serious affair with a neighbour, 'Chips' Lane; while Captain Fenwick became less attentive to the Miss Peels and more seriously involved with Mrs Talbot. 'Need not have troubled about Capt. Fenwick's flirting with us,' wrote Ellen on January 2nd. 'I believe he will be caught on the rebound – in a mouse trap.' Ellen however continued her teasing ragging friendship with Captain Bertie, interspersed with long talks about men, women and marriage; while Mary could neither bring Sav to the point nor break free from him. The main outside interest was Willy, who decided to transfer to the 3rd Dragoons, which entailed two years' service in India. In the meantime he came home to persuade Uncle Roger to pay his debts and during his leave swept his two delighted sisters away for a brief whirlwind trip to Paris. This glamorous interlude however only served to emphasize the dullness of ordinary life. Family relationships continued to be difficult and one can detect in the diary a growing mood of depression and frustration. 'What would I not give for something real to do? I am tired of trying to amuse myself and not succeeding.'

Thursday 6th January
Capt. Cowan came to play hockey. Ice like a ploughed field. We went back to tea with them. Capt. Fenwick came in, he was either very sulky or very shy and we were not gushing.

Friday January 7th
We went over to the Piercys and found them skating on the mill pond. We played hockey, had some rather good games. We

meant to be dignified, but somehow it evaporates at hockey. It is not a dignified pursuit. Telegram from Willy to say he has been offered a troop in the 3rd Dragoon Guards. Hope he won't accept it. They are in India.

Tuesday January 11th

Thawed and rained all day. Uncle Roger wrote. He thinks it would be a good thing if Willy did exchange into the 3rd Dragoon Guards, I hope he won't.

Saturday January 15th

Lily [Piercy] wrote to ask us to come over to luncheon. She is much gone on Chips. The Cat and the Edwards[es] have got up a skating party dinner at the Barracks and a party to *The Mikado*. Dis–gusting!! *We* tried hard to go without success.

Sunday January 16th

Fanny had a cold and got a good lecture about craving for excitement, and that we were all very ordinary young persons and thought too much of ourselves. [This may have been the occasion which went down in the family annals when Fanny, complaining of dullness, was scolded by her indignant mother: 'I don't know what you young people expect. Why only the other day I asked the curate at Marchwiel to come over, *wet or dry*'! He was ever afterwards known as 'the wet or dry curate'.]

Monday January 16th

Teddy [her eldest half-brother, then aged seventeen] and I walked over to the Piercys for lunch. We talked a good deal on the way. He has wonderful good sense. He was thinking how one would feel when dying if one had never done anything but amuse oneself. He is about right. But what is one to do under present circumstances? It is so different for a man. Papa was very cross and Mama preternaturally cheeky all dinner time.

Wednesday January 19th

The Infirmary ball was at Acton. Mama, Mary, Fanny and I went. Mary wore yellow, I dark green and lilies of the valley and Fanny white. Capt. Bertie said it was too hot to dance, managed one or two, not with me. Either it is because he is chaffed or he is tired of me. Capt. Fenwick said he is going to get married but not to the same, he will tell me about it. Sav was unsatisfactory too. I did the Cat once, she rushed up to Capt. Fenwick and told him it was their dance, but I made him take me back first, and the General walking off she was left alone. The Piercys looked nice. Fanny did not enjoy herself much.

Saturday January 22nd
Willy is gazetted to the 3rd Dragoon Guards in India. I don't like it a bit, but Uncle Roger wants to keep him out of England.

Sunday January 23rd
Papa's birthday of 59. He goes just as hard as ever.

Tuesday February 8th
Frost. Went to see Parker the mole-catcher yesterday.

Friday February 18th
Thawed. Papa and I went to Ridley Wood. We quarrelled on the way. Papa said I was a 'spectacle' and everybody laughed at me out hunting and he was ashamed. I quarrelled with Mama when I got home. She deserved it for making mischief, but I *think* I must have been in a bad temper. The Piercys came to lunch. They say everybody calls us by our Christian names, Capt. Bertie *tout court*. They tea'd at the Cowans. Walter (nice boy) told Ethel we were the nicest girls he knew, and hadn't our equals in the country. Mrs Cowan thinks Capt. Fenwick is making a fool of himself with the Cat. Carried *nem. con.*

Saturday February 19th
We walked over to Cefn, found the Palmers and Cecil Slade [a friend of Uncle Roger's]. Mama drove over there too, the Irrepressible [Cecil Slade] much shocked her by calling her 'my lady'. Aunt Milly was charming as ever. Uncle Roger is always the same.

Monday February 21st
Carden. Large meet. They ran up to the hills and we lost them and wandered about, which was very dull, only Mary had a good time [with Sav presumably] but nothing came of it. Fanny and I had our top hats, which excited much derision, but Capt. Bertie did not like mine much. He was very good-natured and took a stone out of Foxhall's foot.

Tuesday February 22nd

The Edwards[es] had their theatricals. First came the waxworks, Chips was showman. First came the United Kingdom, Connie looked ghastly and Muff purple, Muriel Talbot ugly, but Ethel Piercy very pretty. The Sleeping Beauty, Ethel Piercy and Mr Engleheart, was pretty, and Beauty and the Beast, Florence Piercy and Mr Godfrey. But the tableau was 'Italy'. Capt. Fenwick and Mrs Talbot came on in Italian costume, she danced and he played a banjo and sang. We roared till we nearly went off. He saw, and kept staring but could not revenge himself. She looked about 50. Afterwards they had two charades, 'Crumpet' and 'Stagestruck'. Lily Piercy, Mr Howard and Mr Godfrey acted very well in the first, but Mr Engleheart, who acted all the young men in his Sunday clothes and a little rouge, was a good-looking stick. The Cat was a dream of ugliness in a fair wig, I never had imagined that even she could look so hideous. She had a vulgar part which suited her. Capt. Fenwick occupied himself with making faces over the side, till she joined him and they made a little tableau behind. In the second Capt. Bertie was a retired greengrocer, and he acted very well indeed, but read his part. He was capitally got up. Mr Engleheart made love again, his 'Is there any hope for me?' was perfect – as a specimen of frigidity.

Ash Wednesday February 23rd

Letter from Willy, enclosing very nice letters from Sir Dighton Probyn and Col. Curzon. They strongly advised him to take his troop. He has bought us a Persian carpet, nice boy. Thinks he will come home, I do hope he will.

Thursday February 24th

Papa, Mary and I went to Leighton, the North Cheshire. There was an immense field. They found directly and had a 6 miles point to Beeston in 30 minutes, very good. Foxhall went very well but I got thrown out from following Papa by some wire. There were lots of falls, some rather bad ones. Col. Scotland nearly killed me by crossing, several people saw and he was made to apologise, but I am afraid he put the fault on me. Miss Tennant [presumably Margot] got jolly and slapped me on the back. Capt. Bertie told me a lot about the theatricals, he said he and I ought to have done 'At Daggers Drawn'. He was very affable and so was Sav. Rode home about 14 miles by myself.

Sunday February 26th

Bangor Church. We stayed for the Holy Communion. Uncle Roger was there and came to lunch and Mary and I walked back with him to Cefn. Col. Brown, Capt. Bertie, Gen. Mostyn and Mr Engleheart came to tea in the cottage. [The cottage was an ornamental summerhouse on the edge of a small lake in Cefn Park. It seems rather a chilly spot for tea on a February afternoon.] Capt. Bertie told me all about the General's fall, his own fall. I told him about my hat. He teased me most of the afternoon. After tea I told his fortune [by palmistry]. We stayed behind and the others, happening to see, roared. He went on about my fall last year and remembered all I had told him out cub-hunting.

Monday February 27th

I went to tea with Mrs Cowan and we afterwards went for a walk. She asked me about the General and Mary. She thought he liked her and thought it would be a very good thing and I told her all about it. She also wanted to know if I cared for Capt. Fenwick. I should have liked to have told her about his other love affairs, but refrained. She offered to speak to the General. She thinks he is behaving disgracefully.

Thursday March 3rd

We drove over to Cefn and found Gen. Mostyn alone in Uncle Roger's room. I went out to find them and they were left alone. [Ellen's pronouns are hopelessly entangled but what she clearly means that while she went out to find the rest of the company Mary and Sav were left alone, when, she adds: 'They went further than ever.' One would like to know exactly what that implied; certainly not seduction, probably nothing more than a few kisses, but that was quite sufficiently shocking for Victorian days.]

Sunday March 6th

Capt. Fenwick and Capt. Bertie came to tea. He and I consorted as usual. They played the idiots with my bangle and Capt. Fenwick told me I was a naughty girl, and he should put me in the pond. Sav was snubbed as he deserves.

Wednesday March 9th

Meet at Edge Green. I appeared in a new topper which hardly had the success it deserved. Capt. Bertie could not believe it was a new one.

Thursday March 10th

Uncle Roger and Gen. Mostyn came to lunch. Uncle Roger much down about Ireland. [Gladstone had just taken office with a pledge to bring in Home Rule.] Did texts for the workhouse.

Friday March 11th

Had letter from Willy, the Khedive had given him the Order of Osmanlia, but he is very much down on his luck, poor boy, and it is *such* a bad time to apply to Uncle Roger, between Ireland and his liver.

Sunday March 13th

Bangor Church. Uncle Roger came to lunch and to my disgust Mama went on at him about Willy and succeeded in putting him in such a rage that when we began we did not get much out of him. The Irrepressible, Capt. Bertie, Col. Hutton and Capt. Fenwick came to tea [in the cottage at Cefn]. It was so cold we sat indoors most of the time. I finished telling Capt. Bertie's fortune but he snatched away his hand and kept dancing about with my muff. Capt. Fenwick says now, from something he has heard, he does not think he will marry the lady now, she is another widow, a ripper, but he does not think he will like the children. Wanted to know what I thought of it. Cecil Slade and Uncle Roger walked back with us to the bridge. Cecil Slade walked with Mary, gave her to understand how much he liked her, how angry at being left to walk with ME, etc, but as he is not a marrying man it don't amount to much, especially as she does not return his flame.

It would be interesting to know what significance was attached in those days to 'not a marrying man'; Ellen would certainly not have intended it as it would be used nowadays. Indeed it is doubtful if she knew that such a thing as homosexuality existed. On the other hand Victorians sometimes sensed more than they knew. One wonders why Mary Ellen Palmer was so sure that her brother would be content not to marry and to make her children his heirs.

Tuesday March 15th

Cefn. Aunt Milly was charming. We talked about Willy. She will put in a good word for him if she can. Had another shot at Uncle Roger. He says he [Willy] will have £1,000 and ought to be able to live on it, but he was in a much better temper than last time, showed me a schedule of his debts. I believe he is fond of him still.

Saturday March 19th

Willy came home by the 7 something train. He is looking very well and pleased with himself. He has interviewed the ministers and given them his views, written a letter for Cabinet circulation, got into no fresh scrapes and fallen much in love with a Miss Mina Scott at Cairo, a young lady with money, has half proposed and been half refused. [He was probably not too depressed about this. He used to say he liked being in love, 'it made one so comfortably miserable.' When one remembers Archy Peel's agonies over Willy's mother one can quite see that father and son were not formed to understand one another.] He [Willy] is angry with Mama for jacking up Uncle Roger.

Monday March 21st

Smoked with Willy in the evening and talked over his plans. [This was advanced behaviour for the times. Smoking for ladies was only barely taking hold in the 'nineties and we are still in 1887. It also shows how close Ellen was to her brother.] He gets leave till June 14th.

Tuesday March 21st

Went to lunch at Cefn. I walked with Willy and he gave his ideas on regimental ladies. Had a row at breakfast, Mama complained to Papa of Fanny who got well scolded. An awful thing has happened at Cefn, the Palmers found a poor man drowned in the pond. The General [Mostyn] would say nothing but 'How funny'.

Sunday March 27th

Capt. Bertie came to tea. He and I walked down to the cottage together and he asked why I disliked Mrs Talbot and I told him I did not think she was a nice woman. He said she was not perhaps altogether the woman he would marry, and I said I should be very sorry to see any relation of mine – or friend – he added, married to her. He declared he did not think me spiteful but I believe he did.

Wednesday March 30th

In the afternoon we walked to Cefn and Uncle Roger and General Mostyn met us. We had tea in the cottage. Mary and he flirted as usual. They ought to leave off, he is behaving shamefully as he always does. Willy came down with a grave face to smoke. He had been talking to Mama. She does not intend taking Mary and me out this year, says she is tired of it. In fact we are evidently *de trop* in this establishment. I suppose one ought to marry. It would be horrid even if one could, to marry someone one don't care a bit about, but I suppose one must come to that. It is sad, when one thinks of all one's old dreams, working together for some noble aim in perfect concord, but one soon gets '*disillusionée*', especially when one is *de trop* everywhere, and it doesn't mend matters to write sentiment in middling French and English mixed. Willy was much taken with the idea of Cecil Slade [for Mary]. He says he is a thorough gentleman and really 'straight' and it would be a very good thing. He says the General is not, he has heard things about him, though he would not say what, and if he meant to propose he would have done so. I am afraid that is so, and she certainly ought to break it off.

Thursday March 31st

Willy and the Palmers went to Ireland. We went over to the Piercys. Felt all day as if I had had an unexpected dash of cold water in my face.

Saturday April 2nd

Meet at Broughton at 12. Lots of people out. I rode with Capt. Bertie for a long time and reciprocated our ideas about marriage etc. His ideas are less worldly than mine. I can't get over Wednesday and it makes me feel bitter.

One feels that if, at this moment, Captain Bertie had proposed Ellen might well have accepted him, although she was not in love with him and obviously cared more about Willy than any outside young man. Captain Bertie however, although he seems to have been always ready to discuss marriage in the abstract, never did propose; possibly because of lack of money, possibly because his feelings were not seriously involved, possibly because Ellen snubbed him. It was a period when girls, in reaction against Early Victorian submissiveness, thought it amusing to be snubbing and almost rude. One finds this type of heroine in contemporary novels, notably those of Rhoda Broughton. Ellen had a sharp tongue; Captain Bertie was said to be 'the rudest man in the 23rd', which, as she commented was 'saying a good deal', but he probably got as good as he gave. Their chaffing friendship continued: at Bangor Races he is described as being 'very rowdy with the cherry brandy, my flowers etc.', and at the following day's meet he 'gave me a lead and called me to all the best places. He said we were wild animals when he first knew us, but at this interesting point we met Papa and I had to ride home with him instead.'

Any considerations about a possible future with Captain Bertie were however laid aside in the present excitement of a trip to Paris with Mary and Willy. Neither of the young ladies had ever been out of England before.

Saturday April 16th
   Paris is settled for Monday. Papa gave us £50 and a long lecture about being independent. He is very unreasonable.

This may seem a slightly churlish reaction to a gift of £50 but it must be pointed out that the 'gift' came out of the Miss Peels' own pocket. They both had some money of their own from their mother's estate. It was paid to Archy Peel who took most of it in return for providing them with a home, but gave them an allowance. When at a later date Ellen wanted to control her own finances it led to trouble.

Monday April 18th
   Started for Paris with £55 and lots of good advice and cautions and a very kind present of £2 from Mama. Had a cheerful journey though Willy was much annoyed by a bunion, some *café au lait* at Calais and got to the Westminster where we had some chocolate and went to bed, Willy having sternly refused to ask the price. [This was typical of Willy's attitude towards money, as is the next day's entry.]

Tuesday April 19*th*

We went to dinner at the Café Bignon, where there was Alphonse whom everybody knew, he was a spy under the Empire. The iced champagne and the dinner were capital, but the bill, oh what a surprise! was 128 francs [at the then exchange about £6]. We were completely flabbergasted but had to pay and abused Willy.

The next three days passed in a whirl of gaiety: sightseeing, the Opera, the theatre and of course shopping. In spite of her anxieties over money Ellen would plainly have liked to stay longer, but Willy (and this again is typical) 'got a letter from Miss Scott which takes him back on Friday, bother her'. At the end of the visit Ellen summed up her impressions of her brother as follows.

Willy has been a very pleasant companion. He is awfully nice but his temper is rather uncertain, and he is very impatient if one is stupid. Very ambitious, and I don't believe he really cares a hang for M'ss Scott, though he is going back on purpose to lunch with her. He is perfectly reckless about money, but always wants to pay more than his share.

After all this excitement North Wales seemed duller than ever. There was the usual round of tennis, cricket and visits to the Piercys. Ellen went to call on Parker the mole-catcher, who was 'rather wandering and paid me several compliments'. They showed off their Paris dresses, 'which have arrived but don't quite fit'. Sav and Mary 'flirted tremendously' and Ellen 'in a moment of misplaced confidence' told Captain Bertie that she had forgotten to wash her teeth, 'and he went on about it the rest of the time.' Family relations seem to have been worse than usual. 'Mama kept complaining of us all the evening,' wrote Ellen on May 18th, 'and I felt leanings towards step-matricide.' Matters were not improved by the death of Grandmama, Lady Alice Peel, which meant mourning and the cancellation of such slight diversions as the militia dance. Willy, ever hopeful, and now 'very much gone on Miss Scott', anticipated a legacy and 'thinks we shall be about £1,000 better off. *I* think £100 would be nearer the mark.' (Ellen was right.)

Willy was now staying with the Palmers at Cefn. His love affairs, wrote Ellen, 'seem prospering, he has 3 notes, 2 photos, several

relics and unless she is a dreadful flirt I suppose she will have him.'
With his own love life in such a hopeful state he had leisure to concern himself about his sisters.

Sunday May 22nd

I walked back to Cefn with Willy. He was very full of Gen.
Mostyn and Mary. Mama has been talking to him and he heard of
it before. Says she must stop it or he will, if necessary, by calling
him out. Says he evidently means nothing. I rather agree with
him. It ought to end, but in this dullest of all dull places, where
no-one ever comes and whence we never go, what else is there to
do? It is a shame to waste one's time so. One might as well be a
jelly fish.

4

'Something to do seems coming'

Willy's intervention did not succeed in bringing Sav to the point.
'The poor innocent,' Ellen recorded, 'said he had never flirted with
anybody else but would not say he liked her better than any
woman in the world, he said "he never told ladies that", so I suppose there is an end of it.' (This however was far from the truth.)

Meanwhile another possibility had gone whistling down the wind.
Captain Fenwick became definitely engaged to 'the Cat'. Ellen wrote
on June 26th:

> It is true about Captain's Fenwick's engagement. He must be
> rather a cad. If he used to speak so of the woman he meant to
> marry, his 'friends' ought to look out for themselves. I suppose
> he was caught on the rebound but I hate finding people are not
> what you thought them – like Tom Pinch [in *Martin Chuzzlewit*].

Captain Fenwick did not seem to have allowed his engagement to
affect his behaviour.

> *Wednesday June 21st*
> We met the happy pair on Chester station. I congratulated her,
> the others did not. He was exactly the same, wanted to travel
> back together. It was very amusing.

A week later they again met (this time without Mrs Talbot), once
more at a railway station – Birmingham – on the way to London.

> He was *very* mad, he swore he nearly proposed to Mary by that
> stile, if it hadn't been for her temper. Was delighted I had kept
> his secret [about his previous proposal and rejection]. We told
> him that we were very sorry and it would never be the same
> again, but I believe, extraordinary as it may seem, that he really
> likes her. She has been a very clever woman.

The engagement continued to have its ups and downs. In August
'she and he were both talking of giving it up, and she about her

dead husband, having promised him etc., it seemed doubtful.' A few days later Ellen met the Captain at a dance where he was 'more than affable'. 'He thinks much too well of me,' she continued, 'but he ought not to be an engaged man.' Captain Fenwick may have been of her opinion for the last entry relating to him in 1887 describes him as 'a ghost of his former self. They are to be married on the 27th [October]' and 'the less I like it the longer I look!' (This was a quotation from *Punch* captioning an illustration of a horseman craning at a fence.)

Captain Fenwick however (unlike Sav) was brought to the altar. There is a sad little postscript in the following year. The ex-Mrs Talbot was tubercular, and pregnancy and the birth of a baby girl were too much for her. 'I am so sorry,' Ellen wrote, with a touch of real feeling, 'just when she had got what she wanted, it seems so sad and I feel as if we had behaved badly to her.' Three days later she summed up in an epitaph almost Greek in its simplicity. 'Mrs Fenwick is dead. It is very sad, she seemed so happy when she had what she wanted and now she is dead.'

To return to the spring of 1887. Willy's love affair had been going no better than his sisters'. Miss Scott, though occasionally encouraging, seemed on the whole to be inclined to refuse him and he decided to go to India to join his regiment, to Ellen's great sorrow. It was particularly annoying that he left at the end of June just before the girls went up to London for their share of the season. Owing to Lady Georgiana's disinclination to take them about and to their mourning for Lady Alice that was an extremely truncated visit. However in the course of a week they ordered hats in the Burlington Arcade, riding habits at Busvine's, and stays at Madame le Blond. They also went to *William Tell* at the Opera, to see the Kendals and Mrs Beerbohm Tree act in *Lady Clancarty*, 'a lovely play, the prettiest I have ever seen'; to the Academy, where their preference fell on a picture of *Huss* by Lord Leighton; to a garden party at Ham House; to the Wild West Show, and to both the Oxford and Cambridge and the Eton and Harrow at Lord's. After which they retreated to Glenisland, Uncle Roger's place on the river at Maidenhead. This was less amusing than London. Uncle Roger's major pleasure in life was his steam launch and his favourite recreation was to steam up and down the reaches of the river. On great occasions they would go as far as Marlow and sleep there, over a butcher's shop ('accommodation doubtful,' Ellen commented), returning the next day. Uncle Roger was once actually caricatured in *Punch*, a perky little figure on the deck of his launch, scattering the rowing boats to right and left, with the caption 'Captain Jinks of the *Selfish*'. It was not a very sparkling form of entertainment and even here, away from Papa and Mama, Ellen managed to get herself into disgrace. While the others were steaming away, the ubiquitous Captain Bertie came down and took her out in a punt as far as Cookham. 'We had a charming punt, he was very nice, but not a nice reaction when we came home. Aunt Milly was furious because we had taken the Jubilee punt [presumably a new punt christened in honour of the 1887 Jubilee]. Uncle Roger was very kind, but I felt as though I had been put in the corner.'

Uncle Roger was always kind to his sister's children and had a particularly soft spot for his younger niece who, although she was no beauty, must often have reminded him of the lively high-spirited Ellen Palmer; but Aunt Milly and the younger Ellen did not draw well together. 'Uncle Roger came with us to the station,' wrote Ellen, 'and seemed really sorry we were going. Aunt Milly not. She dislikes me very much now. Told Mary we did not get on, that I was assuming etc.' The echoes of this *malentendu* lasted a long time. When in October Mary was asked over to a Cefn shooting party without her, Ellen recorded the information in her diary with the concluding query: 'Jubilee Punt?'

Back in North Wales Ellen's sense of discontent and frustration increased. She wrote on August 30th: 'Mary's birthday and mine, 25 and 24. I feel very old, very idle, very useless, and rather *de trop* altogether.' Family relationships were worse than ever. Papa refused to let them have the horses for cub-hunting because Teddy and Fanny were late for prayers; Mama quarrelled with the Cowans 'and had the cheek to say near neighbours should not be intimate (Mr Peel thought), and that she [Mrs Cowan] arranged meetings for us with the officers! Mama appears to have *no* sense of manners.'

Thursday September 20th

Papa was most offensive again at dinner. Really it becomes almost a question how long one can stand it. I was very angry and life seems sometimes both useless and unpleasant.

Monday September 24th

Had a real row with Papa. He began. I don't know when I have been so angry. I felt I could marry anyone who came handy no matter who, but no-one turns up when one is angry or I could have proposed myself.

There was no one to turn up. Captain Fenwick was married, Sav continued unsatisfactory, and Captain Bertie was eloquent on the subject of not marrying without money. Even the minutiae of life wore a gloomy aspect. Poor old Parker the mole-catcher, whom Ellen had so faithfully visited, died; Lily Piercy, semi-engaged to Chips Lane, could not win his rich uncle's consent and was miserable; while the petty restrictions inflicted by their elders were particularly galling for young women in their mid-twenties.

Monday October 10th

We had a great row about rounders. Papa objects very much and talked a lot of rot about leap-frog and kiss in the ring, calls it a romping game, which is quite absurd.

Monday October 17th

We went to the cookery class in the afternoon. The Piercys were there and we learnt to make Viennese bread, omelette, and Shrewsbury cakes. It was rather fun. Mama boxed my ears before starting, which somewhat surprised me and I complained to Papa, who also seemed rather astonished.

Wednesday October 26th

We went to the barracks in the afternoon. Mama was much perturbed at not being able to keep us all in the same room, and horrified at my being left alone with Captain Bertie in his sitting room! ! It sent them into fits. She was also much horrified at my going with Mr Engleheart to look at his sketches.

Quarrels with her stepmother however, even when they led to blows, troubled Ellen very little. She looked on them as something unavoidable, as it might be a wet day. It was Papa who, because she genuinely loved and admired him, could really hurt her. She was becoming discouraged. The stumpy leather-bound book which had been given her for her birthday in 1886 was nearly exhausted and either a volume has been lost or she got tired of chronicling the unsatisfactory flirtations and family rows. At any rate after November 11th (which records a good run with the hounds, Sav cheekier than ever and Captain Bertie chaffing a good deal) there are no further entries till March 1888, when a new theme is introduced.

March 19th 1888

Papa got a telegram from Willy's Colonel to say he is out of danger and doing well. We never knew he was ill. He said he had his head cut open at polo, but made nothing of it, that was about six weeks ago. It is dreadful his being so far and so long away.

Tuesday March 20th

Willy's birthday. Papa read us two letters from the doctor and the colonel. He has been frightfully ill, unconscious for 7 days, and his right side paralyzed at first from compression of the brain. Poor dear Willy. It is a grain of comfort that he will probably be invalided home. We ought to be thankful he is as well as he is.

There seemed however no immediate prospect of Willy's coming home. The next news early in April was that he was going up to the hills and then coming back to England, as he would not be fit for duty. 'It sounds very bad indeed.' commented Ellen. She was not the girl to leave it at that. The idea of Willy ill and far away with no one to look after him affected her strongly; she thought she and Mary might go out to India to help nurse him back to health. She consulted Uncle Roger, who, perhaps remembering a beloved sister who had come out to the Crimea, was favourably inclined, but to Papa 'the idea was like a red rag to a bull'. 'Papa was so intensely unpleasant about it, that I could hardly begin to forgive him all day,' she wrote. She complained to Uncle Roger but 'though he quite sympathized, he thinks it would be difficult.'

So that idea was squashed and life in North Wales continued much as it always had. The hunting gave way to lawn tennis and cricket matches; Mary had 'another explanation' with Sav, 'which very nearly ended right. *Why* couldn't it be quite?', and Captain Bertie was 'a shade less sulky, but, I don't think much of him now.' Fanny had a penchant for a new young man, Mr Ethelstan, generally alluded to by the girls as 'four figures', owing to his supposed income, and Lily Piercy's engagement was definitely ended. She appeared to be heartbroken, and, when her father died, confided in Ellen that it was at least a luxury to be able to grieve in public. (By the end of July she was engaged 'again', as Ellen wrote indignantly, 'to a Mr Coxon. I was much surprised and think she made a most unnecessary fuss.') There was little news from Willy, except a dictated letter to say that he was getting on well but was in need of money. 'I don't know what will happen,' Ellen wrote, 'he is in debt every 6 months and never even *means* to keep out of it. I should like to help him even though it seems useless. I am sure Uncle Roger won't.'

A spice of variety was a small jaunt taken by Mama, Ellen and Fanny to Oxford. The two girls were taking part in a ladies' orchestra though it is not quite clear how this came about. In their first season Mary and Ellen Peel had been invited to join Lady Folkestone's band. This was a very smart affair, a string band of girls, mostly the daughters of friends and relations, organized and conducted by Lady Folkestone (afterwards Lady Radnor) which gave annual public concerts in St James's Hall. In their second season the Miss Peels' invitation was not renewed, and Papa, characteristically, decided that they must have behaved badly in some way, though Ellen, more reasonably, deduced that they did not play well enough. Whether the ladies' orchestra which assembled in the Sheldonian was anything to do with Lady Folkestone is not stated in the diary, though it seems probable that this was so. In any case the concert 'went off very well. We were all in white muslins, feels stupid in the daytime, especially as we came early and they applauded us.' There was a party in the evening and Ellen sat next to a Mr Capel, who confided in her that 'he keeps a locked diary and writes down everything. I can't. No woman could. He says he is often morbid. I should think that is probably the reason. He is very nice and we rather made friends.'

The next day opened with a more daunting entertainment.

Friday April 26th

Fanny and I went to breakfast with Dr Jowett, as Mama was unwell. It was rather alarming, I kept thinking he would call my remarks silly but he was most affable, talked about men being plucked, causing anyone's death etc. Sir John Conroy, Mr Penrhyn and another man were there. We were shown into a room

with the three alone at first, but it seems that is all right at
Oxford. I feel rather small here, they are so learned and so up to
everything.

Altogether Ellen was dissatisfied with life and with herself. 'I got
a bad fit of the blues in the evening,' she wrote when she was once
more back at The Gerwyn. 'I feel old, and looked upon as fast without getting the fun of it. I would give *anything* to be lovable. The
children are growing up, and I feel decidedly *de trop*. The idea of
Mr Capel writing his diary rather comforts me, but why do I like
people better than they like me, and yet snub them?' Even the prospect of the annual exodus to town did little to relieve Ellen's mood
of depression. 'I do not think I shall like London. I *dread* going, but
everything seems flat.'

Things improved a little once the move was made. The house
taken by Papa, 25 Ennismore Gardens, was a very nice one, boast-
ing of a billiard-room and handy for 'the Harrod stores' and riding
in the Park. The horses (and presumably a groom or two) had come
up from Wales and the cobbled mews behind the high houses, now
demoted to garages or tiny bijou houses, must have echoed to the
stamp of hooves and the hissing of ostlers. Papa took his daughters
to Ascot in turns, though he rather spoilt matters for them on the
first day by insisting on 'taking a bag and sandwiches which
annoyed us very much, but we had to eat them.'

The next day, which was Cup Day, it was Mary's and Fanny's
turn for Ascot and Ellen did a round of calls with Mama. How
many people nowadays remember that ritual? The leather card-case,
the square of transparent tissue paper that divided the bits of paste-
board, the larger card engraved with the lady's name followed by
the names of the unmarried daughters (quite a galaxy of Miss Peels
by this time) and the two smaller cards for the gentleman, since Mr
Archibald Peel could call on both the lady and gentleman of the
house whereas it would have been improper for Lady Georgiana to
leave a card on a man. It was on their return from this not very
exhilarating exercise that they found a telegram from Willy. ' "Re-
quire Mary and Ellen immediately. Doctor thinks it good plan. Telegraph reply. Will be met at Bombay. Bring ball dresses and riding
things." I cannot understand it. If he wants me I would give anything to go. I wrote to Uncle Roger about it. Papa will not hear of

it, and is, I think, unkind and unjust, of Mama that goes without saying.'

Friday June 16th
 I am most unhappy about the telegram, the others went to
Ascot but I would not. I cannot decide on anything. Papa says he
will have nothing more to do with me if I go. Perhaps Uncle
Roger will help.

Uncle Roger however, when he came to London on the following
Tuesday, 'would not advise, and I was obliged *much* against my will
to give it up. I never was more disappointed, it makes me cry when
I think of it. I never thought he would want me and I should not be
there.'
In spite of this disappointment, compounded partly of her genuine concern for Willy and partly, one cannot help feeling, of her
desire to escape from the narrowness of her own life. Ellen managed more or less to enjoy the remainder of the season. Even an
outing to Portsmouth to view the Fleet was not ruined by Papa's in-
forming her, in his usual unkind fashion, that 'she got herself up
like a Merry Andrew'. Perhaps she was getting inured to being
snubbed. The family returned home on July 30th and Ellen wrote,
'We have enjoyed the season, though I don't think we are any for-
rader. Things much the same here.'
'Things' indeed seemed exactly the same until, on August 17th, a
telegram was received from Willy announcing that he was coming
home. 'I cannot understand it,' Ellen wrote, 'as he meant to go to
Australia. Papa and Mama have horrible ideas, about "violence",
"proper supervision" etc., which I cannot see any call for.'
This seems to have been the first time that the seriousness of
Willy's condition was admitted by his family. Papa would seem-
ingly have been quite content to see his problem eldest son voyag-
ing round Australia by himself, without any supervision, but he
was not keen on having him at home. A few days later Uncle Roger
wrote to say that he thought Willy's head was weak 'but the doctor
does not say so. Something to do,' Ellen added, 'seems coming.' It
was coming indeed, though at this stage she was far from realizing
the magnitude of the task.
Willy returned to England on September 8th. Papa went up to
London to meet him and brought him down to The Gerwyn on the

10th. 'Willy is very infirm, wants an arm to walk with, and has not control over one side of his body, which makes him talk and laugh rather thick. It is delightful having him to look after. He is quite sensible but of course rather clouded sometimes.'

It is difficult to assess Willy's condition. He could get about by himself after a short while and was capable of writing, or perhaps dictating, letters, though one cannot be sure how balanced these were. 'Willy wrote a long letter to Gen. Buller about Major Barttelot, about those letters in the papers.' He was physically however far from right, suffering from fits of ague and from sickness. 'Not sure,' wrote Ellen, 'whether it is biliousness or brain.'

In early October the three eldest Peels migrated to Glenisland and it was from there that Willy and Ellen went up to London to see Willy's doctor. Mr (afterwards Sir) Victor Horsley is to this day one of the great names in neurosurgery, and Willy could not have been under more distinguished care.

Tuesday October 24th

Went with Willy to see Dr Horsley. He gives a good account and says he will get quite well, cannot decide on an operation yet. He seems a particularly nice man. He will not allow Willy to stay in London by himself, so we are in a great fix as we must leave Glenisland, telegraphed to Aunt Margaret [Papa's unmarried sister] and went to look at Clarges Street.

Wednesday October 25th

Clarges Street cannot have us so we are going to Storey's hotel. Aunt Margaret cannot have us at all. Willy went out alone and *walked* back at night. Left the Palmers very sorrowfully. Willy was sick.

Thursday October 26th

Willy was very sick and unwell and Martin [his servant] had to go home, so I slept next him, in Martin's sheets, much to his delight.

Friday October 27th

Went to see the doctor again. He says Willy must be kept quiet. Aunt Margaret most kindly came up and helped us very much as she says she will have him at Rickmansworth. Willy and I called on the Scotts and found them at home, Willy went back to tea there. [Miss Scott was Willy's *inamorata*. A few days previously he had taken Ellen to lunch to meet her. 'She is pretty and charming and they seem great friends,' the percipient diarist observed, 'but I think she will be able to take care of herself.']

On October 29th they went down to Rickmansworth to stay a few days with Aunt Margaret, who had obviously taken pity on the rather forlorn pair. Martin gave notice, 'he said he would not stay another night because Willy swore at him so, but they made it up', and Ellen thought it worth recording that she did her own hair, which was an exercise to which she was quite unaccustomed and it was evidently accomplished with difficulty because 'that idiot', presumably the maid, 'had forgotten the curling irons.' A Princess Alexandra fringe such as Ellen wore required curling every day.

Thursday November 1st

Willy and I went to London to Marlborough House. I waited downstairs in Col. Teazle's (?) room, and saw Sir Francis Knollys, Mr Wash and Col. Townsend, felt rather out of place. HRH was very gracious, and Willy told him his plan for getting the earldom of Castlemaine renewed for Uncle Roger. [A crack-brained scheme if ever there was one. The Palmers were certainly not descended from Lady Castlemaine, and only very doubtfully from her first husband Sir Roger Palmer. It says something for King Edward's goodness of heart that he was always very kind to poor Willy.] I got an unkind letter from Papa which made us decide on Eastbourne [which had been recommended by Dr Horsley]. I think of going to Australia with Willy afterwards and have asked for my money. How things change, just when they seem as if they never would.

Saturday November 3rd

Aunt Margaret and I walked to Rickmansworth. They think too much of me here. I think Willy is getting much fonder of me now. I feel rather a humbug somehow, I don't know why, but I think it is Papa's contrasting opinion.

Sunday November 4th

Went twice to church with Aunt Margaret, morning and evening. She talked to me a great deal. It always makes me feel so bad, being with good people.

Monday November 5th

Heard Papa making prompt arrangements for my having my money. He thinks I am going off for good. By Aunt Margaret's advice I wrote him a nice letter. I really am fond of him and don't want to quarrel a bit, though it might be advisable to separate. Aunt Margaret gave me a lovely puppy and I christened him Flick. I am really sorry to leave her.

Tuesday November 6th

Did my hair most successfully. Got a long letter from Mary about separation and Willy's debts, which showing to him I actually succeeded in getting a list of them, and getting him to promise to see Stretton [Uncle Roger's man of business] about clearing them off and starting afresh. We went to see Dr Horsley who gave a favourable report and does not wish to see him for 5 or 6 weeks, so we go to Eastbourne. Then we lunched at the Bachelors' and Willy went to tea with the Minx [Miss Scott] who was gracious.

Wednesday November 7th

Packed up, getting very hot. Mr Stretton came. Problem to raise £2000. He was kind but doubtful, will see Uncle Roger. We lunched at the Bachelors'. I met Julie Stonor in the waiting room [this was the girl with whom King George V was so much in love in his early days], who was most affable to my great surprise. We came down to Eastbourne afterwards. I wonder how we shall like it. Flick was troublesome, made arrangements about him, he is a darling.

Thursday November 8th

Saw all the tradesmen. Eastbourne is expensive. The books will emphatically not be 30s. a week. Took Flick out, and Willy. Responsibility for the first time in my life, and rather lonely.

Friday November 9th

Took Flick out. He was a dirty little animal. Heard from Mary that Papa thinks I am going to draw on my £80. So I wrote to him and to my banker to transfer. [It is impossible to understand in detail all the financial transactions between Ellen and her father; but it is a sobering thought that had she not had her own money, probably round about £600 a year secured to her by her mother's marriage settlement, she would never have been able to get away from North Wales at all.]

Saturday November 10th
Lovely day. Willy went out in a bath chair on the parade.

Monday November 12th
Wrote to Cocks and Biddulph [the bankers] to pay my money to me, not having heard from Papa before. Got a letter from Papa, first rather a nice one, an answer to my first, why couldn't it come before? [Presumably before she wrote to the bankers.] The 2nd thinking I mean to withdraw altogether. As he insists on that if I take my money *I* shall have to withdraw which is a nuisance.

Tuesday November 13th
Willy had his bath chair. Books came in, considerably over the 30s., 'reckless extravagance'. [This sounds like a quotation from Papa.]

Thursday November 14th
Heard from Papa again, we, it seems, pay one third of the expenses, which I call excessive [it would certainly seem so, seeing that she and Mary were two members out of a family of eleven], and he cannot do with less, so I get no surplus but I told him I want a larger allowance.

Friday November 15th
Went to the swimming baths and had a lesson from the English Champion, she said I was promising, so plucky. As she was holding me up in shallow water, I was, *very*.

The days at Eastbourne slipped by pleasantly enough. It is noteworthy how much more popular Ellen became as soon as she was removed from the inhibiting influence of home. There were tea parties with various local families, including the Cavendishes at Compton Place; there were further swimming lessons, and Ellen took a Turkish bath 'a new sensation, rather pleasant'; there were nicer letters from home; 'all peace again, Papa will give me his advice, he says, about my future affairs', Flick, as puppies will, was

ELLEN FANNY MARY

PAPA

sick, rolled in the dirt and made a mess in the night; and on Sunday November 25th Ellen recorded: 'Did not go to church, and felt for the first time that Sunday is a day of rest.' There was, it is true, one black day when three letters arrived: one from Miss Scott to Ellen 'saying all was to be over', one from Mr Combe, the Palmers' solicitor, 'saying Willy was not and never would be Uncle Roger's heir', and one from 'the Commanding Officer at Canterbury, finding fault with the tone of Willy's letters. We burnt all Miss Scott's letters and sent her things back. I think it is a good thing over, and Willy bears all his ills wonderfully well.' There is one other disquieting entry on December 8th. 'Willy has taken to go off walking by himself. I am afraid he has a lot of little friends about. I know of several.' This is the first indication of what was to become the major problem of dealing with Willy. He had always been susceptible but now the balance of his brain was disturbed and he became a compulsive womanizer. Nor was he able to distinguish where his attentions would be welcome and where they would not and he was totally unable to resist the coarsest advances on the part of the opposite sex. For a girl brought up like Ellen in the narrowest of environments, whose knowledge of sex was limited to an occasional stolen kiss, the situation must have been horrifying. It is a tribute to her love for her brother and to the general sanity of her approach to life that she was able to see it for what it was, a symptom of an illness and not a sign of sinful depravity.

Apart from these difficulties Ellen's only other worry at Eastbourne was about her weight. It was always a problem to her: she was short and when she was worried or unhappy she tended, as many people do, to put on flesh. She was horrified to find that she was 10 stone $8\frac{3}{4}$ lb. in her outdoor things and after a Turkish bath was 'actually heavier'. When she returned to London and ordered a dress at her tailor's (Grant's) 'the beast said "I was grown so stout he didn't know me." ' It was however a consolation to go to Dr Horsley's who 'was delighted at Willy's progress and allows him to go to Australia', though even this held its bitterness, for 'Willy does not want to take me now, I am so sorry I don't know why, but I fancy because of St Petersburg.' A cryptic statement which it is impossible to fathom. Her care for Willy did not falter in face of this rejection. On November 10th they went to Cocks's the banker, 'as I am to guarantee Will's £1,500.'

Saturday December 14th

Went to Grant's and tried on my dress, and actually ordered a hat at Heaths', a very pretty one, brown with sable tails. Willy and I went to Cox's and signed the papers. We dined at the Bachelors' and then went to see *Faust up to Date*, the songs and dances were capital. Got very anxious about Willy who did not come in till 1.30.

Sunday December 15th

Willy never came home all night, he makes me very anxious.

Tuesday December 17th

Aunt Margaret came, I was so glad to see her. Then Julia, George and Agnes Peel [her cousins, children of the Speaker], all full of the reversed *valse*. I went to Grant's and then to the Peels as they had asked me. Willy of course forgot his engagement and was not here when Col. Brabazon and Capt. Kendal called. 'Jack' very affable. [Jack, more generally known as 'Brab' or 'Bwab' was one of the great Edwardian dandies. Colonel Kendal, a distant cousin of the Peels', was his brother-in-law.] Everyone says that Willy ought not to go to Australia alone. I am so worried. He is dreadful about women, I hardly knew men were so bad, and London has a most deteriorating effect on him I am afraid to let him go alone. After consulting Hussell I have written to Dr Horsley. [Hussell was the new manservant. As he was provided by Dr Horsley he probably had some nursing experience.]

Willy came home in an angelic frame of mind at 10.30, and announced, after talking to Hussell, that he would take me to Australia. I am rather glad. He is not fit to go alone – but – it will be a great brouille.

The family were not pleased. 'Heard from Papa, Mama, Mary and Fanny. They did their duty,' Ellen commented drily. Dr Horsley took a different view. 'He said the cares were such a strain he wondered how I had borne it and thought it "only right" someone should go with Willy to Australia.' Finally Papa, bowing to *force majeure*, telegraphed his consent and Ellen went down to North Wales to spend a last week among her family. 'I was *very* glad to see Mary and Fanny again,' she wrote, 'also the others' [which probably means the other brothers and sisters rather than their parents].

Life in North Wales pursued its course. On Christmas Eve there was a meet of hounds at which eight of the Peel family turned out. On Christmas Day there was church at Bangor, turkey, rain all the afternoon, the Hon. B. came over and they played commerce in the evening. There were theatricals at the barracks and supper afterwards. The following Sunday 'Gen. Mostyn and Capt. Bertie walked over, and we walked back with them.' The only unusual incident was that 'Mary found a cheque of Willy's for £100 for Mrs H—. It is really disgusting and the worst is anyone could get hold of him.'

So on this uneasy note Ellen Peel, aged twenty-five, who had scarcely ever left North Wales, who had been abroad only once in her life, who until the last few weeks had never done her own hair, or packed a box, or travelled without a maid, said goodbye to her home and family and, with little money, no friends or companions, in charge of a mentally ill brother, set off for the other side of the world.

5

'How I dread the end of the journey'

During the journey out and the first few weeks in Australia the diary's place is taken by long detailed letters to Mary, which, from the very first moment of the voyage, chronicle all the ups and downs of shipboard life. These letters give a vivid picture of Ellen Peel in her mid-twenties. She was on the whole a simple character. Her faults were on the surface. She was quick-tempered, frequently tactless and somewhat snobbish (though not unduly so considering her background and the times she lived in; not to recognize class distinctions in the nineteenth century would have been equivalent to being colour blind). Her virtues were truthfulness (not only in word but in spirit), warm-heartedness and courage.

She had a lively, mobile face, which never photographed well as its charm lay in its expressiveness. She was short and rather plump, and at home she had been told so often that she was plain (Papa was almost certainly comparing her in his mind to her lovely mother) that she had lost much of her self-confidence. Released from her narrow environment and from Papa's autocratic rule, she was able to become her own natural self and when she discovered that this self was for the first time admired and loved, it sometimes went a little to her head and led her into difficulties that a more experienced young woman might have avoided. Two things made her popular: one was her overflowing vitality, the other was her eager interest in other people. Nearly all her descriptions of love affairs begin with the vague words 'He told me things'. In all her relations with the opposite sex however she was protected by the rather naïve but complete innocence that was an integral part of her personality.

In addition to illuminating the character of the writer these letters to Mary give a rather interesting glimpse of other aspects of Victorian *moeurs*. One is the frequent use of slang. 'Awful' and 'beastly' occur only too frequently. Another is the frankness about bodily details. It is true that Ellen is writing to a most intimate sister, with whom she had probably shared a bedroom all her life; nevertheless it is strange to recall that we are still in the nineteenth century, a period that we have mythologized as being so hypocritical that the table legs were always covered up. Ellen writes freely about her menstrual periods, 'my little friend'; about being sick on the stairs, 'Wasn't it beastly?'; about flowing with perspiration; about 'her tummy having retired into private life'. Even allowing for the fact that we are nearing the end of Queen Victoria's reign, and that excessive delicacy was a middle rather than an upper class attitude, this frankness seems more like the eighteenth or the twentieth than the nineteenth century.

RMS *Austral*
January 5th 1889

Dearest Mary,

Left the hotel and got to the ship. It was bitterly cold, Willy kept adjuring me to comfort him if he was homesick. Train full of passengers a level lot they looked. When we got to the *Austral* the fog was so thick we couldn't start. To my intense disgust I found 6 berths in my cabin which is about half as big as Teddy's room, a small family of four and another. My berth is at the top, you have to scramble up a ladder and round a grating, then there is barely room to hold you and nowhere to put anything. I also cut my finger and dropped my money all about which was annoying. The most striking passengers were a lady in red, Mrs Cummings, an immensely large woman, who Willy shows a decided inclination to sit next. Another was a Mrs Walter, rather pretty, rather second-rate, and the untidiest hair I have ever seen. We took our places next the 1st officer, a very nice little man quite a gentleman, of a very old Irish family. He asked Willy if I should mind sitting at the same table as Mrs Walter, as he thought her second-rate. I have met my inevitable old gentleman, a Captain Somebody, of a very tubby figure, but a great Nimrod in his own estimation. Mrs Walters also informed me she was 'too frightfully daring'. Everyone dines in rugs and shawls etc., as it is bitterly cold and the ship can't be warmed. I had to wait to go to bed as my little family was undressing in twos (the cabin don't accommodate more at a time easily). Played my fiddle but too cold.

Sunday

Still fog. We had a pretty good night, though two of my little family are afflicted with a cough, which is annoying. We intend to make the purser move us. The Bishop (of Brisbane) had a service, two hymns, he raced the organ which came in a bad second, 3 bars behind. He has a bald head but makes up for it in beard. Willy introduced Mr Herbert Gladstone, he is very good-looking, has a beautiful astrakhan coat and, contrary to my expectations, seems affable and amusing. [This was the youngest son of W. E. Gladstone, going out to join his family at Naples.] The officer at luncheon seems rather amusing, I don't know his name yet. There is absolutely *nothing* to do on board, so I talked to him for a long time. I hear there are lots of *Rats* about, brutes. Mr Gladstone and Willy both rather admired the lady in red, but Mr Gladstone rather cried off and left her to Willy. He was rather amusing in the evening but much too intent on getting information. Willy introduced a young American on deck. I walked with him a long time, Mr Jackwith. Everyone tells you all about himself on board, there is nothing else to do. Mrs Walter and I played in the evening, hymns most of the time, and a lot of the men came and sang, but it was so cold no one could stay there.

Monday

Dressed by twos, I nearly last. Curling lamps are *not* allowed and reported to the Captain, so one has to be careful. I said good-morning to the Captain for the first time, whereupon he invited me to take a walk. He is rather a nice-looking man and seems fairly respectable. Then I walked with Mr Foster, who is tall and good-looking, but a perfect boy. Willy more gone than ever on the red woman. I also walked with my American, who is seeking for information and thinks me enormously clever, he is rather a nice little man.

We actually started after luncheon, it is calm so far, but!! Mr Darby, the First Officer, told me that Mrs Walter is the daughter-in-law of the proprietor of *The Times*, her husband was disinherited for marrying her. (Under strict promise of not repeating it.) She has five children she is always complaining of, as her nurse threw her over.

Mr Gladstone and the shipowner enlightened my ignorance of

naval matters after lunch, which is so dense that they roared. The purser won't change my cabin, brute. The shipowner, whose name I don't know, is the third man who has told me things, I don't know why I am sure, but there is not another woman on board who opens her mouth, except Mrs Walter and me. It would be amusing if there were anyone one knows, no one has anything to do on board ship but watch everyone else.

Please thank Mama for her letters. *Sick.* It has been a beastly night.

RMS Austral
January 12th [1889]

Dearest Mary,

I left off on Monday evening. Mr Gladstone, Mrs Walter and some more of us played grab, most exciting. Mr Gladstone's voice is *so* like the Hon. B's that I hardly know them apart, and he pretends to misunderstand you in exactly the same way, and laughs at you much the same. Mrs Cummings is making a dead set at him, it is most amusing. I was in an awful funk for Willy but persuaded Mr Foster to cut him out with her, which he most kindly went in and did.

Tuesday 13th

It was nice all day. The purser changed my cabin, there are only two in it now. They are rather a nuisance hunting for bugs and very second-classy, but otherwise unobjectionable. Mr Scrutton (the shipowner), Mr Gladstone and I played fives all the afternoon, it is a capital game. They laughed at me like anything because I asked the Captain (Captain Ruthven) to go and fetch me a fives ball, they said it was perfectly ridiculous in the Channel, but as he went I had rather the best of it. But about four the ship began to roll and I retired to a chair. I forgot if I told you that, besides being friends with the Captain, Mr Darby and Mr Gladstone, I have raised two ardent admirers. One is the little American, named Jackwith, the other is Mr Scrutton. Mrs Walter has also left her place because she says Mr Darby never speaks to her when I am there. But I am the only woman, except her, as *is* a woman and not a nonentity on board, except the red woman, and she isn't respectable. They are a mixed lot – I believe she and some of the men are real bad lots. I never before realized how useful a man can be, *always* seeing you are comfortable all day long, especially when you don't feel well. But alas! on Tuesday evening I felt constrained suddenly to leave the deck, Mr Scrutton jumped forward to offer me his arm, but I couldn't get down and was sick all over the stairs, wasn't it beastly? The night was awful. I was nearly all right, but you had to hold on to the sides of your berth to keep in, and every movable thing rattling all over the ship. Your clothes are all lost, you can't stay packed in with two people in a box all day, there is no one to do anything for you, you must do your own hair, with the ship rolling till you can't keep still and the deadly feeling of faint sickness that comes over you whenever you lift your arms. But I was less bad than almost anyone, man or woman, as the weather has been most exceptionally bad. All Wednesday we lay about the drawing-room, nobody had hardly washed or done their hair, it was impossible, and you could not get to meals, I eat hardly anything for two days but biscuits and a B.&S., as, the portholes not being open, the dining-room was too stuffy for words. Mr Scrutton was my only comfort. He arranged my pillows, found my shawls, and talked to me when I wasn't too seasick. Wednesday night was nearly as bad, and Thursday worse, as the men were below. Mrs Walter was very bad. She has no nurse and her babies on her hands. She looks about 16 herself, a perfect child, with no more ideas than a baby. I try and help her all I can. Our only amusement was a little romance of Mr Gladstone's and Mrs Cummings. He gallantly escorted her downstairs, she collapsed (she is an immensèly big woman), fell on the mat and refused to stir, nearly drove him frantic.

I came down to breakfast Wednesday with about five others. Thursday was better, still very rough, but our sea legs were beginning to grow and we got up on deck and I got down to luncheon. I actually offered to sleep with Mrs Walter's children, she was so bad and I was nearly all right, but she wouldn't. She is rather a dear little thing, very small, rather pretty, knows all the comic songs in England and always singing them with appropriate action, and very fond of me. Friday we were practically all right again though it was still rough. I walked about the deck all day with Mr Scrutton and Mr Jackwith in turns, they both told me their affairs. I am evidently a new type to the American and he is much impressed. I believe we stayed on deck much too late, but it's stuffy below and our cupboards are not inviting.

Saturday

Played fives all morning with the same lot. I am getting quite a swell. Mr Jackwith has confided to me in strict confidence that Mrs Cummings is a bona fide adventuress, and they say the man with her is a thorough blackguard. They keep their distance from me. Mr Scrutton says I take care people do that and that everything I do here is right because all the others will imitate. Shows them to be a level lot, doesn't it? He says he knew me at once for a 'county family', and that he supposes I never in my life met a Radical and a tradesman, as he calls himself, before. He is very nice, tall, good-looking, clever, knows an immense lot, and — hopelessly in love with somebody else. He *is* useful to me here, does every mortal thing for me all day long. I didn't know of the lady till yesterday, and I am the only person he has told but one man.

We had a lot of music in the evening yesterday, rather too much. I took a farewell walk with Mr Jackwith, and I shall draw a veil over our parting. He wanted badly to find a quiet corner, but luckily there wasn't one. He kept half hinting. Finally he said there were many things he didn't think it right to say now, but he knew he should meet me again. He had to leave at Gibraltar, he couldn't come on. I don't think anyone has ever liked me so much before. We got to Gibraltar on Saturday, at night unluckily, but it was fine and a lovely sight, the squadron was lying there. Where the waters of the sea and the ocean meet there is a distinct line, but it is so unlucky we can't stop anywhere because of that fog to make up time.

The red woman was deader on Mr Gladstone than ever and he flies in abject terror. She has made him lend her a handkerchief, they all say he is a great fool and she will show it everywhere. Mrs Walter tells him she will protect him. I never laughed so much; they were sitting on a seat, Mrs Cummings edging towards him and he retreating till he nearly fell off. She gets so loud all the men hate her now. She was bent on one of them taking her ashore at Gib., I was so afraid she would get Willy but he had too much sense. All the others would help me too with anything of that kind. Mr Scrutton and I remained all the evening about. There isn't much chance of either employment or company, but everyone is immensely civil to me, and Willy says I am a success on board ship. Strikes me I am getting egotistical like Fanny's little friend. I am looking forward most anxiously to your letters. It was awfully nice on board this afternoon, sunny and warm, (I am in my yellow shirt which is much admired) and when I come on deck my particular friends, having nothing better to do (fancy a man in that predicament!) find me the most comfortable corner, chair, rug, etc., settle themselves and talk, and they really do it very well. Oh if Harrington [nickname for Fanny] and you, 4000 [Mr Ethelstan], and Fencock [Captain Fenwick now replacing Sav] were here, *their* days would be numbered, as if a man likes you he is done here. Mr Gladstone is only most friendly all round, he is, I think, intent on higher thoughts and fleeing the red woman, I am ashamed of liking a Radical so much. Mr Foster is a charming boy, so good-looking and always ready and very clever. You will be sorry to hear I wore my teagown once, and fancied myself much, but Willy was horrified and made me promise never to wear it again. Mrs Walter thought it lovely, but it seems it is not quite the right thing so I feel rather small, only I boss the show here, so it doesn't matter. I am dying to hear from you.

Private: January 13th

This is strictly for yourself. I am feeling horribly blue today. I wish you were here. I feel such a beast and I can't make up my own mind and I hate writing. On Sunday evening Mr Scrutton said he should like to part with me completely at Naples, you can guess why. Because, he said, supposing what was utterly unlikely, I should have to give up too much. He is a business man, and working like a horse for his father, they have to tide over something, and lives near London, and our habits and everything were dissimilar. I do like him so much – somehow he misunderstood me, and asked me yesterday for another half-hour. He cares for me much too much, it has made me feel miserable all day. I shan't tell you all he said, but he wanted me to take 6 months to decide, or any time, but I couldn't. I don't love him, though I like him so much, and I expect when he is gone today I shall feel awfully sick. He said decide now, tomorrow it would be too late, in ten minutes it would be too late. He said he purposely spoke coldly, he wanted my head to decide, he despised a man who could not keep from hot animal wooing. Of course, he says, he knows no one I know and he would never be Mrs Anybody's husband, his wife must be his wife. He is a *man*, which so few men are. One thing weighed against him very much, he doesn't believe. But you know one is grateful to people for caring for you like that, especially when one feels rather lonely. Then when we had quite settled we talked of Willy. Of course they all know he isn't quite right, and I believe they have been very good about it, he and Mr Foster and Mr Gladstone. They have choked off that woman, but now there are two regular legs aboard, who want to gamble. They have not tried Willy yet, and Mr Scrutton says Mr Foster watches him as a cat does a mouse, and if they do he will speak to the Captain, who has full powers on board. Everyone is going away today, Mr Scrutton, Mr Gladstone and we are left with the riff-raff and *such* a lot. I like Mrs Walter very much, she is so graceful and has such a pretty voice on deck. In the middle of the conversation she and Mr Gladstone came up and danced a jig, it was too absurd. Do write and sympathize and don't tell me I have behaved badly. I do sincerely trust that nothing of the kind will happen again, but there is no one else for them to talk to and they like talking to me. I can hardly believe I was such a blind idiot when I wrote you the other letter. The last thing he said last night was did I trust him enough, if I ever changed, to let him know? not to let him think 'she changed her mind and won't tell me', so I said I would. Of course Willy knows nothing. I *shall* feel deserted after today. We get to Naples at 3.

Your affectionate sister,

Ellen

If ever he can do anything for me or Willy he said just ask him to do it, without feeling it gives him any claim.

RMS Austral

January 16th [1889]

My dearest Mary,

I was horribly disappointed to get no letters from you at Naples. Now I shall get none till Australia.

We got to Naples yesterday, the bay is too lovely, and Vesuvius was flaming. The sun came out in the afternoon and it was perfect. Nearly everyone went on shore. I was going, but Willy suddenly came down on me like a thousand of bricks, saying I never knew how to behave, that that teagown was the root of it, that I wanted to go about by myself, of which I hadn't the faintest intention, etc., all on the deck, and I couldn't keep the tears out of my eyes which was beastly, though I don't think anyone saw hardly. [It seems almost incredible that Willy, seeing how he had behaved and would behave in the future, should adopt this highly censorious line. Probably he was jealous of Mr Scrutton, and perhaps his weak and wavering morale was a little stiffened by the fact that he felt he was, or should be, responsible for an unmarried sister. It is of course a caricature of the double standard of morality enforced by the Victorians, and would be comic if it were not so sad.]

I did settle to go with Mrs Fox afterwards, but it seemed hardly worth while the trouble then, so I stayed, and Mr Scrutton got back his things and stayed too, till the last possible moment after dinner. We were alone together all the afternoon and for nearly a quarter of an hour after dinner. He does love me so. I feel exactly like Jo in *Little Women*, as if I'd murdered something and hidden it. I tried to choke him off. I don't know what possessed me but as we were leaning over the rails, I told him we looked as if we were going to be sick over the side, and that I liked him much better when he didn't make love. He was so angry, he said it was a cruel thing to say. The night before, when it was all over, he asked me to give him the evening as it was the last, and afterwards he thanked me for it. I can't tell you what a beast I feel. He says if I were in his own rank of life he would never give me up, that ten years ago he could have offered me a good position, but of course we were in different sets and I should have to step down. He says he shall hope for years, and that he will never forget me but always hope to be some use to me.

Mr Gladstone went too, we were awfully sorry to lose him, they, Mrs Walter, young Devitt, Mr Foster and I were always together and we had such fun sometimes. When they were all gone and Mr Foster had a pal and we were alone, we felt awful. It was cold and gloomy and I could have howled. Poor little Mrs

Walter told me her troubles. She is such a child and such a little fool, and has married the wrong man, poor thing. A lot of fresh people came on board, a very level lot, I think. I walked with Mr Foster on deck and he tells me that some of the leg's confederates have come on board and there is something up. I am anxiously waiting. He says he thinks Willy has taken their measure and won't have anything to do with them. We shall be lucky if we get safe without a row on board, there was very nearly one, for Mrs Walter loathes Mrs Cummings, so that there is every prospect. I told her so, but Mr Scrutton only said I should be quite certain to be out of it and you may bet I shall, it would be like fighting a sweep. Mr Foster is so nice, but he looks frightfully ill [he was tubercular], that lovely pink colour and his eyes are so bright. Today ought to have been perfect, going through the Straits of Messina, but it is pouring, and you can't see anything hardly. We passed Scylla and Charybdis today. The weather is quite a miracle of badness they all say. I do miss having no one to find out always what I want and fetch or make up a game for me. My faith in Scott is shaken, I could have sworn my face would be my protection, and it isn't. Mind you marry Fencock, I am dying for news. One of the new men on board is a Mr Fenwick, cousin of the one in the Blues, he doesn't seem bad, but an unpolished individual.

Tuesday

Very rough. I played bull with the Captain who is rather a nice man. The game is to throw weights on a board with numbers marked on it. To my great surprise he spoke to me very gravely about our having stayed on deck when the lights were out. I had no idea it really mattered, but it seems it is not considered proper, though why you should on a beautiful night go down to a stuffy box at 11 o'clock beats me. However I have solemnly promised not to do it again. We had a concert last night, Mrs Cummings in a flaming yellow and black dress, dirty torn lace and bedroom slippers was too objectionable for words. She was so rude to Mrs Walter that it was all I could do to keep her quiet. I have not my music, so can't play, but you will be surprised to hear that I am much in request as an accompanist. Last night was awfully rough, the highest wind we have had, really the Mediterranean is a fraud. There is hardly anyone at meals, I am one of the best sailors on board. The Captain says he never knew such persistent bad weather. I had a long political argument with the Bishop yesterday on the disestablishment of the Church. He told me I was an advanced political thinker, and had evidently studied the question. Do you call that nothing?

It is baggage day. The steward found and appropriated all my methylated spirits [used for curling her fringe] and the stewardess smelt them this morning in my cabin. I shall have to use eau-de-Cologne.

Sunday

Went to church, hardly anyone else did. We steamed slowly up the Canal and saw real live Arabs and camels. The captain invited me to come to his cabin and look at his photographs, which is a great honour I believe, at least he was most afraid of the other women seeing. Mrs Walter proposed herself and came too. She is very nice, I need hardly tell you that she tells me everything and I tell her nothing. She wants badly to find out if Mr Scrutton proposed. So do they all, they had a bet about it, but I fancy they think he didn't.

I forgot to tell you I have been telling everyone's fortune, with the most startling success, it is quite uncanny. Do you know the elder Scofield had death marked in his hand quite plain (I didn't tell him), the other had a fall on his head which nearly killed him, and Mr Foster's destiny, which was originally very good, is quite rubbed out. I feel like a witch rather, and also as if I were on a tightrope. We got to Suez. The Canal was lovely by moonlight and the other side lit up by the ship's electric light. Mr Foster and I said all the poetry we could remember to it, which wasn't very much.

Monday

We got up early and all went on shore for a donkey ride. I was late and missed them but Mr Foster kindly came back for me. It is an unpleasant process landing. You are fought over by a dozen dirty Arabs, one of whom takes you up and carries you in his arms ashore. They seemed to find me awfully heavy and I bet I am, we eat all day. The donkeys are named Jubilee, Mary Anderson etc., they are rather hard to stick on. A very good conjuror came on board but he wouldn't do the mango trick. He insisted on showing me one if I wouldn't tell the 'mashers' as he called them. He called me alternately 'Mrs Langtry' and 'Mrs Consul'.

Tuesday

A Red Sea day and fairly hot. Have done nothing all the morning, shall do nothing all the afternoon. I told Willy all about Mr Scrutton yesterday. I am glad I did, he was so pleased at the confidence. He prosaically remarked that I shall always have someone to fall back on. He didn't seem to mind the idea of the connection as much as I expected and fully agrees he was a real good sort. I gave Mrs Walter an awful lecture on the folly of her ways yesterday, which she took very well. The Bishop also pastorally advised her which made her angry. Madame Cummings has left for ever. She inveigled the smallest man but one on board to go ashore with her, a mild little man, an awful fool. After dinner, rather to my surprise, Mr Fenwick came and talked to me, about religion and his own affairs. He doesn't believe. It is so sad hardly any man seems to now, (but he believes in *woman*). I like him now, as Fanny said, he isn't such a cad as I thought. [This refers to a remark of Fanny's much quoted in the family. Passing judgment on some young man, she said: 'He's such a cad,' adding reflectively, 'he never speaks to me'.]

Wednesday

Hot again. The men played cricket and I played lawn tennis with the Captain, and then with Mr Foster and the bishop. The bishop in tights, his apron, no coat and Jaeger flannels, dancing about the court, looking quite indecent when his apron blows away, you can't help feeling he ought to keep his legs covered, is a lovely sight.

Thursday

Fairly hot. Played several singles with the Captain, he then invited Mrs Walter and me to his cabin and sprinkled us with scent and gave us each an iced champagne cocktail, it was perfectly delicious. He was in such a fright of anyone's seeing. Mrs Walter declares he likes me awfully but my face will certainly be my protection this time. I talked for hours to Mr Foster, he is so surprised at the books we used to read, Locke, Berkeley etc. Told Mr Fenwick's fortune with my usual success, he quite believes there is something in it.

Saturday

Comfortably warm. Played cricket a little, they are awfully impressed with my play. It is slightly slow on board. I like Mr Foster very much and talk to him for hours but –. If you were here with the man of your affections what a time you'd have!

Tuesday

Hot. They have delicious ices. I perspire nearly all day and all night and yet manage to grow horribly fat. The same men get your chair and things, there are always plenty of them, being so few ladies. We dressed for dinner on Monday, the first time, my old black hit the mark exactly. The Captain had us *privately*, *very* privately into his cabin and gave us (Mrs W. and me) an iced champagne cocktail again. They are delicious, we have them last thing before dinner. We all painted programmes for the sports. I did a little picture of the ship on mine which was much admired. I did them for my own particular friends and put their initials on them. Mrs Walter and a lot of them sang glees on deck, till the Captain sent 'his compliments' and 'it was eleven o'clock', to their great indignation.

Wednesday

Finished the programmes and they had sports in the afternoon, all sorts of jumps, cock fighting, scratch pulls and all sorts. The 2nd class joined. They had a ladies' race, mercifully my feet are so swelled it made a first class excuse. *Nothing* would have made me run, I would as soon recite the 'Curfew'. I amused myself by pumping Mr Foster about a medical case on board, when I had made him tell me I laughed at him and he was simply furious, but laughed at himself. He is such a nice boy and does everything for me.

In the evening we danced and played in turns, we had some first-class polkas and quadrilles, the Captain polkas beautifully. I am so sorry for him, he is a disappointed man (he told me about it) and he would be so good-looking if he hadn't a red nose (doesn't that appeal to you? how is Sav?), large dark eyes, a very good figure and a face which sees a good deal.

I have just heard from Mr Foster there is a doubtful lady in the 2nd, she is pretty and I am afraid for Willy. He was awfully bored yesterday and I feel as if I had been neglecting him. We got to Colombo today. I got up early and saw a coral reef and coconut trees and all sorts yesterday. I feel *that* travelled.

Much love to young Harrington and the boys, I can't help my letters being stupid.

Yrs. affec.
Ellen

RMS *Austral*
February 1st [1889]

Dearest Mary,

Got to Colombo. Most people went ashore after luncheon. The deck is all over coal dust and the cabins are stifling as the port-holes are shut which is a distinct nuisance. I stayed for Willy (being afraid to let him go alone) and so did Mr Foster, and we went onshore about four with Captain Ruthven. It is a lovely place. I never saw a tropical town before and it was a dream of beauty, especially when the sun set over the water. We went to see the cinnamon gardens and then came back to dine at the Grand Hotel, where we had a very nice dinner, and then went for a walk in the dark through the town. Capt. Ruthven talked to me a great deal and we discussed the same subjects, men and women, marriage etc. – you know – he is rather nice but has had a thoroughly disappointing life. Mr Foster and I went back to the ship because he didn't want Willy to sleep ashore, nearly every-one else did. The port-holes were shut because of the dust and I never spent such a night. I didn't perspire genteelly, I simply *flowed* all over. I felt awfully virtuous as Mrs Walter had offered me a share of her nice cool room ashore.

Friday

Everything black, dirty and hot. We went away (I am writing this a week later). Nothing particular has happened. [In later days Ellen re-reading this letter added a marginal note: 'It did, only I didn't know it, but for Mr Foster there would have been an awful row. The purser was very angry.']

We play lawn tennis every afternoon and they play cricket. I am marking some handkerchiefs for Mr Fenwick. Mr Foster does every single thing I want all day and after he goes down to put Willy to bed I always talk to the Captain. They are put down to me here, everybody nearly is labelled to somebody, I mean the respectable ones. The Captain has been endeavouring to stop an incipient flirtation between Mrs Walter and the 4th officer, he actually sent him to bed last night for sitting in a dark corner with her. The Captain told me this when I was sitting alone with him and it struck me as so funny I roared with laughing, because he is so virtuous, and everybody says, though he doesn't know it, that he flirts with me. The 4th officer is a nice youth and the most awful flirt that ever existed, he tried it on with me last night, but as it is baggage day and he has been getting all my things out for me, I shan't abuse him. You will think I am getting very vulgar but there is nothing else to tell you about. The standing rub here is the 2nd class. They give dances and people, especially Mrs Walter, will go, and the Captain hates their mixing. I think he is quite right, there is scarcely a decent person there, but he is rather sore about it. There is a pretty girl there and some of the men will go, Willy was induced to at first but Mr Foster stopped him. What I shall do when we part I don't know, he manages Willy beautifully, I have no trouble at all. Sometimes I so dread getting off this ship and being adrift again that I could cry with fright. Willy has been very nice but everyone sees that there is something wrong of course. Mr Scrutton thought it awfully hard on me having no man, he would have come on if he had been able. However I daresay it will all come right, I won't let myself be frightened or homesick. When I feel it coming on I hate it so.

Saturday

I marked handkerchiefs all the morning and talked to different people. The men played cricket and we played lawn tennis in the afternoon, the Captain, Mr Foster, Mr Elder and I. Mr Fenwick went to the 2nd class because everyone was talking to someone else. I asked why he didn't talk to me, they said I always had a row ready, and then they all began chaffing Mr Foster, the other men say he daren't call his soul his own and encouraged him to do what they call 'rebel', but he says he contradicted me twice and that is enough to show he can and he won't again. It is true that he never talks to anyone else when he can talk to me and always follows me everywhere, but he isn't a bit in love I am thankful to say. I think he will very likely come home in the same ship, I hope he will. We danced after dinner. The Captain dances the polka better than any man I know, he is in a great fright of being talked about if he dances more with one than another. There is a very nice boy on board, a Mr Elder, they call him 'Young Depravity' because he is so precocious. There is a large Colonial family on board and their twang is something awful, the Colonial accent is far, far worse than the worst Cockney one I ever heard.

Sunday

My foot was so bad after dancing I had it lanced after breakfast. There was an early celebration on deck which I got up for. Mr Darby and the 4th officer were watching it from the bridge in a most profane spirit. They showed me afterwards how I got up and how I knelt down, how untidy my hair was at that early period etc.

We get to Albany today, Melbourne Sunday, and Sydney Thursday about. I shall be sorry to be adrift again. There was the most lovely sunset two nights ago, I never saw anything like it, from the palest green to the most fiery crimson. It is quite cold again down here, I am wearing my black cloth dress today. I do hope you are having good sport. How is Fencock and 4000? and how is all getting on, flourishing I trust. Willy wants to stay in Cairo on the way back, I am not sure. I do hope the Carringtons [Lord and Lady Carrington. He was Governor-General of New South Wales] will have us when we get to Sydney. I feel this letter is simply drivelling but I can't help it. I enclose one to Mama as it saves the stamp and she might read yours.

> Your affec. sister,
> Ellen

How are Flick and Spot [the dogs]?

Tuesday February 11th

A girl called Miss Massey came on board at Albany, an old flame of the Captain's, they all say I shall have to take a back seat now, but she is engaged to be married. We played lawn tennis in the afternoon and danced in the evening. I was most of the time with the Captain who told me lots of things (he told me all his love affair, I think it is the saddest I have ever heard). He is much annoyed with the idea of 'that brat', as he calls the 4th officer, flirting with Mrs Walter. However the evening did not end peacefully. Mrs Walter and I strummed on the piano till eleven o'clock, and when we went to say goodnight to the Captain we found him in an awful rage because we were so late, I have never seen him so angry. We apologized humbly, but it was no good so we went to bed.

Wednesday

I tried in vain to make up with the Captain, he wouldn't, so I got angry, and when he wanted to and asked me to play lawn tennis, *I* wouldn't, which made him furious. We played hopscotch all day, it is a fine game, Mr Fenwick is the best at it. Mr Rogers made me play all my pieces, 'Simple Amen', Raff's Cavatina etc., he tells me where I go wrong, it is fine practice. Sat with Mr Foster all the evening.

Thursday

Got to Adelaide. Got tired of sulking and made it up with the Captain. We did not go ashore. Had some music and some bearfighting, only with the Captain, Mrs Walter and Miss Massey; he is very nice, of very good family, Lord Ruthven's, Scotch, and would be so good-looking if it wasn't for his nose. Captain Castle took a group of us, Capt. Ruthven, Mr Darby, the 4th officer, Miss Massey, Mrs Walter and myself, and gave us each a copy, a nice souvenir.

Friday

More music, a little more bearfighting, and as usual much conversation with Mr Foster. He likes me very much indeed, but luckily that is all I think. He ought never to marry, poor boy. He has been so kind. How I dread the end of the journey.

6

'Papa is the only man I can NOT get on with'

The RMS *Austral* put in at Melbourne on February 14th 1889, six weeks after leaving England. Ever since the gold discoveries of 1850 Melbourne had grown and flourished enormously. In a book called *Glimpses of Australia* published in 1896, its principal thoroughfare is described as follows:

> Throughout the whole length is a series of mercantile and provincial palaces. There is the immense pile of the Equitable Insurance Building, claimed to be the finest building in Australia, the great bank buildings, the offices of the *Argus* and a host of other splendid buildings. Up the centre runs the double line of cable which extends far out into the suburbs and binds every part of the city in a mesh of rails and cables. Altogether a magnificent street is Collins Street of Marvellous Melbourne.

A contemporary engraving bears out this description. It shows Victorian architecture at its wildest and most unchastened – enormous Italianate *palazzos*, French *châteaux* complete with *tourelles* and balconies, classical pediments which resemble those of London clubs, a couple of Gothic spires, and a clock tower something between Big Ben and the Venice Campanile.

Saturday February 15th
We got to Melbourne yesterday but too late to go ashore. There was a drunken row on board last night. We have some of the most awful men on board you ever saw and they got drinking in one of their cabins. They got that poor boy Mr Foster looks after and he got dead drunk, he collapsed outside my cabin and threatened to be sick and they carried him to bed. They woke us all with their noise; the Captain said he would have given £5 to have caught the ringleader and put him in prison for the night.

He was a horrid Jew, who tried to scrape acquaintance with us. Mrs Walter actually danced with him once, but I lectured her so severely that she dared not do it again. He came up to us once: 'What,' said he, ' 'Opstotch at this hour!' Everyone stared and no one answered and he really felt snubbed. We always call him ' 'Opscotch'. Mr Walter came to fetch Mrs Walter. She told him directly she didn't love him and they immediately began to quarrel about going ashore, sounds well doesn't it? She said she was coming on to the ship again but never came. Willy is dreadfully afraid of my seeing her on shore. Captain Ruthven took Miss Massey, Willy and me to the play in Melbourne this evening. He treated us *en prince*, champagne at dinner, paid our railway tickets and play tickets, and we had a lovely moonlight sail to the ship and back. They acted *Sweet Lavender*. The men were good but the ladies awful sticks and such dresses I never beheld. The ladies in the stalls wear bonnets and in the dress-circle ball-dresses and low at that very often. We went back and I slept in Miss Massey's cabin as she was afraid of 'Opscotch coming back drunk.

We four went on shore again and to church, very long sermon. We lunched at a Scotch hotel, very good lunch. Melbourne is exactly like an English town, you could fancy yourself in Wrexham. Then Willy and I went to call on the Lochs, and with some misgivings presented Mama's note. [Lord (at this time Sir Henry) Loch was Governor-General of Victoria. Lady Loch was a sister-in-law of Mama's sister, Lady Victoria Villiers. Ellen's misgivings were due to the fact that she had never got on at all well with any of Mama's relations and had always particularly disliked the Villiers children who were about the same age as the young Peels and were frequently held up to them as examples. However on this occasion all went well, the Lochs were kindness itself.]

They pressed us to go and get some clothes and come back to stay, Lady Loch has further invited me to bring anyone I like to sleep. There's for you. I see myself doing it. Oh the trouble I had to pack my cabin trunk. If the 4th officer hadn't been perfectly angelic – he got my boxes up, unscrewed them himself, helped me to unpack, and Miss Massey also – I should have been done; everything was dirty, lost or crumpled. We got off at last, just missed the train and got here in time for supper which they have on Sundays, on account of the servants, who are the great people here. Capt. Keith Falconer is the aide-de-camp and Mr Fort private secretary. He was most awfully civil, came all the way back to the train to show us the way. The evening was slightly dull though they were all most kind.

Monday

I put on my pink cotton and looked tolerably respectable for a wonder. Lady Loch seems really fond of Mama, there's for you! She seems about the kindest woman I have ever met. Unluckily for us they are going back to England nearly directly. Mr Foster took Willy to see Dr Maudsley in the afternoon, who is wonderfully clever. He was rather depressing. He 'thinks' Willy may get all right, says he has an extraordinarily good chance, but refuses to say for certain whether his brain will ever quite recover. Also he says that, though it is improbable now, bad symptoms may come on, which would probably take the form of convulsions. In that case I should have to bring him home immediately to be operated on. Now what I am going to tell you is strictly private. Mr Foster came here this morning and I had a long talk with him. What all the doctors are afraid of, what in fact his recovery nearly hinges on, is avoiding women. Twice on the ship, I only knew this morning, he was on the edge of a mess with two women no better than they should be, and Mr Foster only just stopped him in time. (One row I do not know the particulars of, but the purser was very angry.) Also before I came out he had arranged to have that London woman meet him at Naples. I trust you entirely not to repeat this. This, as you may think, is alarming. Hussell watches him like a cat, but Willy periodically quarrels with him, he threatened to leave us on Sunday. Mr Foster is kinder than I can tell you. He is going to travel back with us on the *Cuzco*, I think the *Ormuz* is full. Lady Loch is most kind and only anxious to help us. She has written to Lady Carrington and is going to give us a letter to the Governor of Tasmania. Everyone thinks mine an awfully responsible position. So do I. People have been awfully kind to us, though I daresay you think I ought not to mention all this. I *must*. It is no use shirking one's position, but what annoys is that now, when I am vexed, I can't help

crying. It is very peaceful here but dull. I have been twice to Melbourne today, once by myself to see Mrs Walter and once with
Lady Loch. I like them both, Lady L. immensely. Some people
came to dinner last night, Colonials, rather nice, they are different from us somehow. It is just nice here, a mild heat. Everyone
goes in tram cars. I believe Miss Massey will be a very nice
acquaintance, she knows everyone in Sydney and we get on capitally. She gave me her address.

Tuesday

The Carringtons have just telegraphed to say they can't put us
up. It is most annoying. They are up country and have only got a
small house, I suppose that is why, unless he was annoyed with
Willy. [It is not clear what Ellen meant by that last sentence, she
certainly at that time had no conception of the real reason why
the Carringtons refused them hospitality. The truth was that Mr
Fort, the Lochs' private secretary, found out 'a most unpleasant
thing' about Willy. He did not tell the Lochs or Ellen but he
wrote to Rupert Carrington who acted as his brother's private
secretary. What exactly was the mess that Willy got into remains unknown, for when Ellen did eventually learn about it she
told Mary: 'I am ashamed to write it down. I will tell you when I
get home. It is not revealable.' What seems probable is that during their stay in Melbourne Willy was in danger of being arrested
for rape or attempted rape. The laws in Australia were very strict
at that time and if a charge had been pressed Willy might have
been hanged.]

I got one of the nicest letters I have ever had from Mr Foster
this morning ... I think we shall go on to New Zealand and
Lady Loch says she will give us a letter to the Governor of Tasmania, Sir Robert Hamilton. There has just been a dinner party
here, Captain Castle and the Bishop came, I was quite pleased
to see them. I rather like Mr Fort but he and Capt. Falconer
are always hopping about after some old lady. Oh the miseries
of packing and deciding where to go. Willy's spirits and temper
are mercifully very good, but occasionally he gets nasty, not
often. Love to the Piercys and Mrs Cowan. I will write when
I have time to Harrington and everyone,

Your affectionate sister,

Ellen

Lady Loch thinks it perhaps a good thing for Willy not to go to the Carringtons. If only they had not been going they would have kept us.

Willy and Ellen rejoined the *Austral*, which must have felt like coming home, for the three days' voyage up the coast. The next letter to Mary is headed 'Grosvenor Hotel, Sydney'.

Wednesday February 20th

Said goodbye to the Lochs. Lady Loch was so nice, she kissed me several times, and Sir Henry is as kind as he can be. They said if only they were not going we could have made our home there, how nice that would have been. I got such a nice letter from Mr Foster, he said he knew what a trial it must be, and my position is so difficult I must never scruple to ask for help. I went to see Dr Maudsley again as he wanted to soften down his words. He says they are only improbable contingencies and Willy is, and probably will go on, improving, but still now he is not always responsible. Mr Foster came back to lunch, we went into a shop and had an ice on the way. The Lochs sent us down to the ship and he came to see us off.

[For those a little shaky on Australian geography it may be pointed out that the *Austral* approached Australia from the south, stopping at Adelaide and Melbourne and resuming her journey to Sydney.] Willy got £50 but Mr Foster made him give it to me. Hussell is to watch his correspondence for fear of women. When Mr Foster went I was so sorry, he has been so kind. He is coming whenever and wherever I want him if I send, and you can't think what a relief it is. Mrs Walter came to see us off. Capt. Ruthven and I sat on deck after dinner. He began by telling me all sorts of things but stopped abruptly. I don't think he ever means to make love again, poor man, I don't wonder. Willy was so nice in the evening. He says he is so glad I came out and that he considers me a *succès fou*. But I say such silly things to him sometimes, I have so little management, and when Mr Foster is gone there is no one to put it right. Mrs Walter came to say good-bye to me. I am very fond of her and she is awfully fond of me, but she would shock most people and Willy won't let me go and see her on shore. I believe she will get on all right with her husband.

Thursday

Tried my packing. Tell Harriet [presumably the lady's maid] that she will have to give me a lesson when I get home. We had our last game of tennis, a Colonial young woman, who got on at Melbourne, played with us. The accent is something too awful. 'Plie!' she always said for 'Play', and then 'A-out! (out)', and all through the nose. She called the Captain an old beast because she could not take his ball, but I believe that is nothing out of the way. I wept over everybody in turns, the Captain most, Mr Darby next, and, as Mr Foster had asked me, gave Mr Elder all the good advice I could think of. He is only nineteen and so ashamed of his scrape the other night, he is such a gentlemanly boy. Some of the brutes on board tried to make him drunk and unfortunately succeeded. They say it is so hard for a boy to keep straight out here. He is going to write and tell me how he gets on.

Friday

Got to Sydney. The harbour is perfectly magnificent, not a bit exaggerated (I shall endeavour to describe it to Mama, not in your line). I wanted to sleep on board but Willy wouldn't, so we went to the Grosvenor Hotel. Alas for the Carringtons! They say it is comfortable for a Colonial hotel, but I asked for a curtain across my window, there were none (you must have the blinds down or be quite visible), for linen sheets, there were none but cotton ones, inches thick, for a bath in my room, 'No'. So I have left off asking and accept with equanimity the fact that the chambermaid don't take much interest in me and the hall porter, with an amiable smile, sits down while I talk to him. My endeavour here is to let Willy out of my sight as little as possible.

Saturday

Went to the *Austral* to get my luggage and finish packing. The boxes were beastly contrary about shutting. I am sorrier than I can tell you to leave the *Austral* and be on our own hook again.

Sunday

Sydney is very like a large Richmond. We went to service in the cathedral, it was hot, I simply ran. We went to the Masseys in the afternoon, it was lovely going across the harbour. I upset

my tea over my green dress. They only have tea here on Sundays
– because of the servants.

Monday

We went to see Dr Chisholm in the morning, Dr Bagshaw came
too. He said much the same as the others, they will none of them
say out here that they are *sure* Willy will get quite well. I think
he is a good deal better. They say we should leave Sydney soon
because of the heat, so it would have done no good if we had been
asked to stay. Willy said today he thinks he would have liked to
marry me if I hadn't been his sister, I was quite pleased. Lord Carrington has asked us to dinner, Lady Carrington is not here, he
comes every week. Mr Rupert Carrington wrote to say he was
coming to see Willy and has put him up for the Club. I am sorry
as he gets away from me and he was quite happy.

Tuesday

Went to the steamship office and nearly settled to go by Melbourne to Tasmania. Lady Loch has given us a letter to the Governor's wife, and we hope to start Saturday. Capt. Ruthven came to
lunch and afterwards Willy went to sleep and I went for a walk
with him, very improper wasn't it?

Wednesday

It was too hot for words. I did some shopping in the morning
and got so heated I thought I should have died. In the evening we
dined with Carringtons. Oh the trouble of getting your things
ironed here and doing your damp hair! (I have had to turn back
my fringe), but I put on my pink dress and Willy was quite
pleased. Do you know he says that if I were anyone else he thinks
he should like to marry me? There's for you! and yet I am always
at him and don't let him have a penny to keep. There was no one
there but Lord Carrington, his secretary (very good-looking) Mr
Wallington, his brother and one other man. He apologized for
'Lily's' absence, she had sent me all sorts of messages, it was so
good of me to take them in the rough etc. He was most kind to
me and he is so good-looking I nearly fell in love with him. [Con-
temporary photographs of Lord Carrington show him as plump-
ish, with very thick dark hair and a heavy dark moustache – perhaps the admired type of looks in those days?] He said he admired

me so for coming out, women were always so loyal and good, and if he could do anything for us etc. He 'armed' me to the door, I curtseyed to him, he squeezed my hand in both of his, and so we parted. He gave me seats for the opening of Parliament, it was most imposing. I sat between the Premier's and Attorney-General's wives, one was rather nice. I had the best seat after Lady Carrington's, in front of everyone else, and the only armchair. We go to Melbourne on Monday by the *Arcadia* and then to Tasmania where we hope the Hamiltons may turn up trumps. It was so hot last night I contemplated fainting in bed, but thought better of it.

Your affectionate sister,
Ellen

The Arcadia
March 4th [1889]

Dearest Mary,

Thank you so much for your letter, and please thank Fanny for hers, and the nice long account of the ball. It don't seem to have been a highly interesting one, I don't think I missed much. Poor Harrington [Fanny], how disgusting about 4000. I was highly interested to hear about Fencock. I think I should let him slide if he is so disconsolate, there are plenty of nicer men in the world. I am afraid my powers of description cannot be so good as I have always flattered myself. Mr Scrutton is not *much* like Miss Schlenker. [This was the Peels' somewhat depressed Alsatian governess who had been with them from time immemorial. Ellen once got into a row standing up for her, 'she is so bullied'. Mary's surely slightly catty comparison very naturally rankled.] He [Mr Scrutton] was over 6ft. high, good-looking, his manners reminded me of Cecil Slade's. [Uncle Roger's friends, Ellen used to say, had a particular way of talking to a woman, a sort of chivalry, as if it were a special honour even to speak to her. Although this manner had quite gone out with the young men of her own generation, *viz.* Captain Bertie, she found Mr Scrutton an exception.] He looked after you in just the same way, and everyone but me thought him conceited. I like him *very* much though not well enough to marry, but as he is going to wait two years I might possibly do so still. We left the hotel on Saturday. It is a funny place and they are a rummy lot, some of them. We got to know some of them and the ladies (at the hotel) take the whole cake. Several of the men are in the *Arcadia*, there are one or two decent ones, Col. Staunton and a Mr Forbes, whom I took on because he is so like Mr Cooper [of the 23rd], he is my young man for two days. We go over to Tasmania tomorrow, they say we shall like it. Sydney was altogether too hot. I saw a great deal of the Masseys and liked them very much. Capt. Ruthven and Mr Darby put in a lot of time at our hotel, I *am* so sorry to think I shan't see them again. Mr Darby used to tell me all the gossip of the ship, Capt. Ruthven never could think where I heard things at first, and then he used to tell me his ideas of it. They had just been having a row, and each (of course under secrecy and not knowng the other had told) told me his view of the case. Then Mr Darby used to tell me Capt. Ruthven's past history, and as he (Capt. Ruthven) had told it me himself I had an excellent example of the difference of our own views on ourselves and other people's! I had a most touching farewell of both of them. Mr Darby spent the last evening with us and Capt. Ruthven the afternoon before and came to see us off here which was awfully nice of him. I say 'us', but Willy always gets out of the way because they always talked to me. Willy and I went to call on Lord Carrington on Tuesday, he couldn't possibly be nicer but it's a great bore they can't put us up, perhaps they may when we come back to Sydney.

I had a hunt all over Sydney for my laundress who wouldn't bring my things. I got into a tram and got out at the wrong place, I got a hansom and couldn't find it, I never got so angry in my life. Willy was all right all the time, though Hussell told me that one of the women from the *Austral* was looking out for him. I have been asleep nearly the whole time here [on board the ship between Sydney and Melbourne] being bored, but it is very comfortable to sleep on deck. Some of the people on board are very funny. I heard a Colonial lady doing the honours of London. 'Rotten Row,' she said, 'in Hyde Park? Oh yes! that's where we go to see the nobility droive!' and all so beautifully through her nose. It is beastly expensive being at hotels and Willy's illness has cost a fortune in different ways. Much love to everybody, ain't I good to write so much?

Your affectionate sister,
Ellen

Tuesday

We went to see Lady Loch yesterday. She is *so* kind. She couldn't ask us to stay here, she said she was so sorry, but she asked us to spend the day, so here we are. There is only Mr Fort besides, Sir Henry has gone to the races. She called me Ellen, and treats me as if I belonged to her, I am so fond of her. Mr Foster came to see us on board yesterday and we saw him again today. He goes with us to Hobart, I am delighted, he takes all the trouble off me. I made acquaintance with all the officers on the *Arcadia*, they are nice, but not so nice as the old lot nearly, I don't care for the captain. I rather liked my little friend Mr Forbes, he would have liked a small flirtation but I wasn't in the mood and snubbed him, but he runs all my errands just the same. Nothing would satisfy Willy this morning but to go round the world, luckily they won't exchange our tickets. We sleep on board, which is awfully kind of the purser as we don't pay. We leave tomorrow, small boat, I expect we shall be sick.

Your affectionate sister,
Ellen

The scenic aspects of Ellen's trip were 'kept for Mama' who did not preserve the letters. We cannot tell from the next letter to Mary, headed 'Orient Hotel, Hobart, Tasmania' whether Ellen shared Anthony Trollope's good opinion of the place. Visiting Tasmania a few years earlier, Trollope wrote: 'Views can be had which would make the fortune of any district in Europe.' Ellen's concerns were more personal and she had more to worry about than the views.

[*Undated. Sheet missing.*]

Lady Hamilton is not nearly such a *grande dame* as Lady Loch, in fact she reminds me forcibly of Mrs Lees [a North Wales farmer's wife] but she is immensely kind to me. Willy likes this place, it is such a relief to me you can't think. He is really better I think, but it is never safe to leave him alone as he can't keep his temper if anything annoys him. I can never tell you how kind everybody has been to us. Everyone we have met has been more than kind, except Capt. Andrewes of the *Arcadia*. The purser very kindly allowed us to stay two extra nights on board, and he had the cheek to ask me at breakfast what we were doing there. I was so angry. The officers all said it was too rude of him, but it was no use trying to make a silk purse out of a sow's ear. I felt very bad that morning. It was awfully hot, I had to go to Melbourne to see about the steamer. Willy was cross, Capt. Andrewes insulting, I did not know what Tasmania would be like, we had not met Mr Foster, and there was not a soul to help except the 2nd and 3rd officers, who I made friends with, and Mr Forbes, who were all most kind. Mr Forbes and the 3rd officer carried my things down and came to see us off. Mr Forbes is staying here and everyone knew them. The average Colonial girl I detest cordially. She is self asserting, pushing and has a detestable twang. But some are very nice. They all say Capt. Andrewes did not mean to be rude, it was only his bad manners. I was rather pleased to hear from Mr Foster that Mr Elder, the boy I told you about, liked me so much. It seems he thought all the world of me, and when he got screwed was so dreadfully afraid of what I should say, he wanted to stay in his cabin all the rest of the time for fear I shouldn't speak to him. Mr Foster thinks it will keep him straight. I do hope so, he is such a particularly nice boy. I write all the twaddle that comes into my head, I hope you don't mind.

Friday

I have been having such a *beast* of a time. We went to the dance on Wednesday, I put on my pink dress and some flowers that Mr Foster gave me, men were rather short, but Miss Hamilton and a friend of Mr Foster's, a Cambridge man, introduced the nicest ones to me, and at first I rather enjoyed it. Then to my horror I saw Willy prancing about with a very bold looking woman, and soon after Mr Foster came up and told me in horror what she is. She is a real bad lot, though a lady by birth, thoroughly bad. Willy knew her before in London, she got to the ball by mistake and Willy had already promised to see her home, you know what *that* means. There was only one thing to be done, Mr Foster went himself, sort of made love to her, he is very good-looking, cut Willy out by standing her whiskies and sodas, and we got Willy off to bed. She asked Mr Foster to see her home; Dr Webster says she never leaves a man alone out of sheer devilry, and not only that, but she has a husband, a professional boxer and a thorough scamp, who would kill any man if he could whom he suspected. We settled Willy must go away and I packed my boxes, but no, he won't stir, he says it is only because Mr Foster wants to travel with me. He has promised not to see her again, but it seems he deceived us at Melbourne and precious nearly got into a row about it, which we never knew of, till another man told Mr Foster about it. Only one thing would have made it worse and that has happened. I have given Mr Foster more pain that I can hardly think of and then sent him away, as once Willy has got that idea into his head he is no use to him. I never knew before, I thought I was as safe as in Denbighshire, but they all say I never encouraged them. I missed Willy yesterday and tore up to Government House, he wasn't there, I was so miserable I told Lady H. the rest (she knew part, everyone saw it) and she is going to help us all she can by always planning for him, they all recognize it is illness. Mr Foster and Dr Webster think it awfully serious, but may God help us for no one else can do much. Of course Willy knows nothing. I swore just before, really believing it that he did not care for me, he hid it on purpose.

We saw no more of Mrs Lewis as her husband turned up the night of the dance and was heard to administer corporal punishment in the carriage. If he had found Willy at his house as he nearly did!

Hadley's Hotel, Hobart
Wednesday March 29th [1889] (Willy's birthday)

I gave him a small token of my esteem. Much to my disgust he got a note from *that* Mrs Lewis asking him to come and see her that evening. He burnt it and did not go so that was all right. We went to a *conversazione* at the Museum in the evening, and of all the dull entertainments! The Hamiltons were there and a Mrs Fish, who invited me to what she calls a 'rough and tumble' entertainment at her house on Thursday. Went to Government House for a sketching club, and made a lovely mess. Lady Hamilton is curious, she dissects her feelings out loud to me.

Friday

The 'Egeria' gave a dance in the evening. There was a scarcity of men. I got plenty of partners, though once I sat out two, as one man had to go and the other never turned up. There were a lot of pretty girls there, the room was very well done up and the

WILLY

ELLEN

floor capital, but it is very stupid dancing with a lot of strangers and some of the men I knew never asked me! They are a level lot here, you make the same remarks and answer the same questions to each, and they waltz so abominably slowly. I got very angry with everyone for being so dull, and my foot hurt, and I got so tired that I got into an abominably bad temper and actually spoke quite crossly to Dr Webster. I never felt so ashamed in my life, a man I hardly knew and who has been particularly kind to us. I apologized afterwards and he said I was different from last time and he didn't think he could have done anything and we made it up. Willy got on very well, he danced the Lancers and actually tried a polka with me, he got half round several times and did not come to grief at all, he was so pleased.

Saturday

I had promised to take Mary Hamilton out riding, so most unwillingly got up and went; Willy declined. Her family turned out to see her set off, they evidently considered it a most dangerous undertaking, in fact she told me her little brother didn't expect to see her brought home safe. She was in a dreadful fright of her horse and conferred with the coachman most of the time over her shoulder. In the evening we went to the 'rough and tumble' at Mrs Fish's and I had the honour of playing about 4 rubbers of whist with the Premier of Tasmania; he is the Premier though his wife drops all her 'h's, but one learns not to mind that sort of thing. He approved so much of my play that they sent over a note this morning to ask us to go and play again which Willy insisted on accepting, much against my will. We went to church yesterday and then out to luncheon. The hostess, with short hair, a red face, and a large cameo brooch, was most kind; the gentleman next me ate cheese with his knife in his mouth but was otherwise inoffensive. I heard from Mr Elder, he seems to be doing very well, I am so glad. We went to tea and supper with the Hamiltons. I am getting quite fond of them. Lady Hamilton says she doesn't think Willy quite responsible for what he does always, but he is *pounds* better bodily and I think in every way.

Tuesday

Willy is always making plans for the summer but I don't think the doctors think he will be well enough, or fit to be on his own hook. I like this place all right generally, but sometimes I hate it, and though Willy is so good about everything, his plans are sometimes a little wearing if one is in a bad temper. I heard from Mr Foster yesterday, he blames himself for speaking. How I wish he didn't care for me as he does. How is F.? By the by Mama wrote today, a nice letter, though I am sorry to hear that the figure in the Australian liner, in the *Graphic* of February 2nd, had a too familiar companion. Swear not to mention it, but there was a Mr Nisbett on board the *Austral* and he did sketch Mr Scrutton, Mr Foster and me, and I think some other men, but I was lying in a deck chair and cannot call to mind that any of my companions were over familiar. It was a pretty sketch and I was to have it, but Mrs Cummings persuaded the little fool to leave the ship with her at Naples. Also I am surprised to hear that you did not think my letters fit to meet my Mama's eyes, though glad you have been so nice to her as it seems you have been.

Wednesday

We supped at Government House and then I opened the servants' ball with a polka (you may have heard it) on my fiddle. Then we thought we would make a night of it and went to a party at the skating rink which I rather liked. But Willy made up to Mrs White a great deal more than I liked and from all I hear she isn't much. He got a note from her this morning, I looked at it through the envelope before he came, but he did not show it to me, and I am afraid he did not tell quite the truth about what was in it. Also there is a housemaid here, but Hussell says she won't have anything to say to him, and I don't suppose he means anything. It is dirty work, and I do miss Mr Foster.

Much love to Fanny and yourself.

Your affectionate sister,

Ellen Peel

My dresses and habit are much admired here.

Hadley's Hotel

March 31st [1889]

Dearest Mary,

We have done nothing in particular these last few days, ridden, been to a concert, a pianoforte recital, etc. I like some of the people here very much, and I was much amused by Mrs Adams, wife of a judge and one of the leading members of society here, telling me how nice 'we' all thought my manners were, how nice I was to everyone, so different from Lady Hamilton, who it appears is not at all popular here. It must be rather aggravating, as she is most kind and civil to strangers and takes no notice of the local ladies. Some of the girls here are dreadful. One, a Miss Weston, has been worrying me to go and see her (Willy's friend Mrs White introduced her) so at last we went. Two mortal hours did we spend in her company, the only redeeming point was her excessive vulgarity which was quite amusing. She cautioned me not to put up my parasol as it meant a 'disappointment', told me of anonymous presents from 'the men' etc. And we could not get away because of the trains.

We go back to Sydney by the *Oonah* on Friday. How I dread the journey! But I found Willy in someone else's bedroom with one of the chambermaids the other morning, and Hussell says he often does that and is much too much in the pantry and that they are beginning to laugh at him, and altogether we had better move. How I hate the packing and the bustle! I do wish the Carringtons would ask us to stay, but they haven't yet and I can't think why they don't, unless he really was affronted with Willy and I don't think so, he was so civil and kind. Willy is so much better you would hardly believe, but he still does not talk like he used, seems to be sort of sleepy or irritable and doesn't seem to see the consequences of his actions, though he talks far better and more connectedly than he did. His latest fad is taking the hall porter of the Grosvenor as his private servant, he is bent on it. I am glad we are leaving, some young woman left a photograph here for Willy this morning and he would not show it me or tell me anything about it. I expect to be so sick and there will be no one to see after me for the first time.

Love to everybody.

Your affectionate sister,

Ellen

Got no letters last mail, I trust it won't occur again. I invested in a copy of the Feb. 2nd *Graphic. How* like my dear Papa to say it was me, with a man's hand on my shoulder and such a cad's! Unluckily it is evidently a P.&O. ship, as there are Lascars and punkahs on it, which the Orient don't have. (The photo turned out to be from the youngest Fish girl, about seventeen. Willy hadn't asked for it and was horribly shocked, but her mother did not mind a bit.)

Grosvenor Hotel, Sydney
April 8th 1889

Dearest Mary,

Here we are again. Friday I packed all the morning and we said some more good-byes. The Adamses are very fond of us and say we have won golden opinions in the colony! Think of that!! Here too Lord Carrington said I should be received in any manner with the greatest enthusiasm (I had proposed coming out as a chambermaid), we are swells in Australia! My satisfaction in leaving was much enhanced by a note to Willy I told Hussell to open, it was from another woman to make an appointment with him, so we tore it up and he never knew. It makes me rather sick as you cannot think what a watch I have kept on him. Hussell told me it was quite time we moved.

We embarked on Friday night and I draw a veil over the time till this morning. Suffice it to say that I left disgusted at my fatness (Tasmania makes everyone fat) but arrived here thin and genteel. Willy says it was purgatory, it certainly *purged* one thoroughly, but I think it was worse. We got back here at 6 this morning, I think I shall settle in Australia, I shall never have courage to embark again. Several people have written to their friends for us so we ought to be well off. There are a good many people here, and in the first hour I met them I was asked whether I was going to live here, what ship I came in, where I came from, whether I played, and strong hints given for my name. Being rather snappish and still feeling swimmy, I asked one lady why she asked? It shut her up but she didn't seem to mind.

Wednesday

Two or three men have called on us, among others Mr Cartwright, a lieutenant in the *Calliope*. They are perfect heroes here now, they are begged to attend the theatre, are photographed on all occasions, and otherwise annoyed. (I suppose you have heard of the hurricane?) [On March 16th 1889 a hurricane broke over the Samoan Islands where seven men-of-war were lying in the harbour of Apia. The English ship *Calliope* managed to steam out

and so escaped with the loss of her anchor and her boats, but the
German and American squadrons were totally wrecked. The Ger-
mans lost 96 officers and men and the Americans 104.] Willy and
I went to call at Government House yesterday, Lady Carrington
was unwell and lying down, but Lord C. left a deputation to
come and see us, and invited us to take 'pot-luck' with them
tonight and go on to the theatre afterwards. We refused because
Mr Cartwright (one of the officers in the *Calliope*) was going to
dine with us, so he most kindly invited him too which I was glad
of. It was a sort of public occasion as you will see (I enclose
account). The officers of the *Calliope* were all in uniform, and the
principal actor (Rignold) called for three cheers for them in the
middle of the piece. Lord Carrington was much cheered going in
and out, I felt an awful swell as we walked in (I strutted) to 'God
Save the Queen'. Lady Carrington is pretty and nice and a very
great lady, I *think* she is in an interesting condition as her dress
didn't fit, and he was in that peculiar state of fussiness about her
which I know so well. [Mama's constant pregnancies had given
Ellen a quick eye for such things; Judith Carrington was born in
the following September.] Perhaps that is why they haven't asked
us to stay, which disappoints me rather, though they have been
most kind sending us back in their carriage etc. I saw people here
whispering over their newspapers and looking at me this morning, I felt much elevated. By the by why do you say I never
write? I do nothing else. We are thinking of going by train to
Melbourne, I don't think I can face that awful transit to Tasmania again. I liked Mr Rupert Carrington better last night, 'cos
why? he took more notice of me.

    Love to Fanny and everybody.

Your affectionate sister,

Ellen

    Did I tell you of my struggles to dress yesterday? Nobody will
do anything for you here, I had to go out, buy an iron, heat it at
my curling lamp and iron out my own dress, which had been
packed three times (twice by me) since we left, and it really
looked quite nice. [This may not seem a very Herculean effort today but it must be remembered that this was 1889 when all ladies
had maids. Mama during the course of a long life never once put

on her own stockings.]

The Peels were now running rather short of money and disappointed of an invitation to Government House were forced to move to a boarding house.

> 137 Macquarie Street, [Sydney]
> April 18th [1889]

Dearest Mary,

As the Carringtons won't ask us we came here, which is a boarding house. I would not live in one for £1,000 a day. Hot, messy, beastly cooking and all crowded together in one small room where you are expected to make conversation with the landlady, her daughters and the other boarders. Willy was so bored he went out by himself in the evening, with what results you may guess, the old, old story.

Friday

Willy had a touch of fever and ague, thanks to his nocturnal expedition and we sent for the doctor. I am disappointed, I hoped he was cured of the ague.

Sunday

We went to tea on the *Calliope* with Mr Cartwright. She is all trick again. He gave us a lovely tea, lots of chocolate, and me a lovely Samoan fan, he is a very nice young man. We saw the great Capt. Kane. His name is 'Harry', and the joke is that in the late storm the elements said to him 'Hurry Kane!' He answered 'Am I Abel?' (able). Willy went to bed to keep off the ague and I went to church.

Monday

Mr Foster turned up unexpected. He told me something I did not know I will tell you when we get home, but I think I know why the Carringtons don't ask us, but don't you hint you know, it is not revealable. Willy wants to stay at Cairo on the way back. Every week I can keep him from London I consider a gain, as he means to go in for the season, and Mr Foster says he will not be fit to be responsible for himself. We do not call at Colombo on our way home, I am so sorry, I meant to get your presents, there are lovely things there and nothing here but second rate London things hardly.

Tuesday

I am in greater perplexity than ever. We went to tea on the *Orlando* today with Mr Portal. [Alaric Portal was a nephew of Sir Wyndham Portal and an exact contemporary of Willy's. They had known each other since Willy's midshipman days.] Afterwards he [Mr Portal] took me aside to speak about Willy. He says it was an awful shock to see him, he thought he was drunk. He says he certainly ought not to go to London and we ought to strain every nerve to keep him out here. He said he would speak to Mr Foster and get Captain Hammill [the Captain of the *Orlando*] an old friend of Willy's to speak to him. And everything is far worse than he knows. We have been on the brink of open disgrace several times, Mr Foster told me things I never knew before. But Willy is really getting better only he is no more fit to take care of himself in London than anything, and he expects to go there and do the same as ever. Of course this is all *private*, I only know myself on sufferance.

Wednesday

Mr Foster went to Mr Portal and told him everything, with the pleasant addition that Willy has insulted one of the servants here and the landlady spoke to Hussell about it. I want, if they agree with me, to take a little house far away from town, with *no* woman servants or only one old one. Mr Foster told Mr Portal everything, his feelings for me etc., and he says it is impossible for him to stay with us, and it would not do for us to have any man, as people would talk. Mr Portal came to see me last night when Willy was out, he talked over everything, we had to go to the Park and sit under the trees in the dark and, as he remarked, I suppose everyone thought we were making love. He has been so kind. Finally we settled that he is to get Capt. Hammill of the *Orlando*, Lord Carrington, Dr Chisholm, Mr Foster and himself, and they are to speak to Willy, to tell him that going back to a London life now would probably mean madness, he must stay out here. If he won't, and insists on London, they say he will have to be put under restraint (I believe this is impossible) which of course I want to avoid at any price. They are to try and find a man here who will take charge of him if, or rather when, he

breaks out. I am waiting now for the results. Nothing has happened, Capt. Hammill never came, he could not, and the mail is
going, I shall let you know as soon as possible if we come by the
Cuzco or not.

Your affectionate sister,
Ellen

This was the last letter to Mary written from Australia. In place
of the letters Ellen once more started to keep a diary.

Thursday April 18th

Waited in most of the day for Capt. Hammill. Went to the
Carringtons to play lawn tennis. I spoke to Lady Carrington
afterwards and asked her to help us. She was very kind and sym-
pathetic and promised to help. I had to explain more or less.
Capt. and Mrs Bosanquet, Mr Portal and Mr Cartwright dined
with us at the Grosvenor and then we went to [two illegible
words] where Mr Foster joined us. He and Mr Portal spoke to
Willy afterwards. Mr Cartwright and I stayed inside till quite
late, then I came out and coaxed him to stay, till he promised,
thanks to Mr Portal. I was so glad but it didn't last.

Sunday

Mr Portal and Mr Foster came in the morning and talked over
matters.

Saturday

Mr Portal came quite early and then went to Lord Carrington's
and came back. He has heard something which has changed his
mind but won't say what, so Willy has taken it into his head to
go by the *Cuzco*. Lord C. has written to Uncle Roger, he is strong
against our staying, the consequences of that sort of thing are
very bad here. Mr Portal stayed to lunch and we went for a long
walk together and he brought me home. He is *so* kind. Mr Foster
came in the evening. I think after all that has passed his goodness
makes me ashamed.

Easter Sunday

We went to church on the *Orlando*. Willy introduced Capt.
Hammill. I went to early service at St James'. I am so sad about it
all.

Monday

Willy saw Dr Manning the mad doctor here and Dr Chisholm. I saw them afterwards. He says he does not think Willy will ever be the same man again, that he will have to travel with a medical attendant for a year and a half about, and that the Army is doubtful. It is *horrible*, was he saved for that? I have never really doubted before that he would get quite well again. If he does not what good is his life to him? If he would only turn to the other but he does not really believe. Do I? We went to tea on the *Orlando*. Everyone is most kind, but what can they do for him? And he does not realize or know it, I can hardly bear to hear him making plans for the future. I still have a grain of hope in Dr Horsley's opinion. He said he was *sure*. I went to Lady Carrington's, she was most kind but no one would encourage our staying out. If he would only get well again I do hope I shall be able to stay with him wherever he goes. Mr Foster came in the evening and we read Gordon's poems [Adam Lindsay Gordon, the Australian poet]. I went for a walk in the Gardens, I never knew what real sorrow was before.

On April 26th Willy and Ellen went by train to Melbourne to join the *Cuzco* for the homeward voyage. Mr Portal was left behind but Mr Foster accompanied them as he too was returning to England.

Wednesday April 25th

Mr Foster met us at the station, and we passed a most uncomfortable night. He is just as fond of me as ever – unluckily. We got to Melbourne where Mr Fort [the Lochs' private secretary] had taken rooms for us. New complications. Dr Maudsley and Dr Webster don't want Mr Foster to come with us. They came to the play with us and abused him for looking so much in love. [The play was *The Yeoman of the Guard* and the description of the poor 'merryman moping mum Who sighed for the love of a lady' must have seemed only too appropriate]. Of course they think first of him, and everyone else has been thinking of me, which makes a difference. Willy went out in the evening and I couldn't find Hussell and got thoroughly frightened so I *asked* Mr Foster to come with us next morning and of course he came. I know I am sacrificing him to Willy but what can I do? and he promises to flirt with someone else on board the ship. Dr Webster and Dr Maudsley came to see us off. It was too ridiculous, all knowing we knew what each other thought and pretending we didn't.

Although Ellen continued to keep her diary the story of the homeward voyage is best described in an immensely long letter to Mary from the *Cuzco*, dated May 26th and posted at Naples.

Dearest Mary,

It has been no use writing for ever so long as we take the mail ourselves. Thank you so much for your letter. I am so glad to see it seems to be coming all right, but sorry 4000 seems no further. People are very slow in Denbighshire, I am coming more and more to the conclusion.

You must not say that Willy is disgusting, it is simply a form of mania, well known to the profession and of which Willy himself is nearly unconscious. Poor boy, he has been so ill these last days, internal cramp and indigestion. He was in his cabin, fed every ten minutes, for 4 or 5 days. We took it in turns to sit up with him, Mr Foster and I and some of the men on board, but he is all right again, but there is another affection, a rupture I believe, which I think he will be treated for when he gets back to London. On the whole I have not been really sorry for either as we had grave cause for anxiety in other ways before.

This short sentence is amplified in the diary:

Sunday May 6th

Mr Foster told me that Willy has begun again. It is too annoying, an actress in the second class. Must watch him like cats.

Tuesday May 8th

Mr Foster cut in again with the lady, he says she is respectable but stupid. It makes me sick to watch Willy and hear the sniggering about him. Mr Foster has cut Willy out, we can be easy about it.

Friday May 11th

Fresh bothers. Willy has actually insulted a lady here, a Mrs Smerdon. Mr Foster talked to him but the thing itself makes no impression on him, only the consequences. It will be so hard when we get home.

Saturday May 12th

Willy won't apologize to Mrs Smerdon so I did, but it was disagreeable as I had hardly spoken to her before. They all think him off his head and he has such a bad name. It is very, very hard, especially on him.

It is no wonder that these details were not confided to Mary, who thought Willy 'disgusting'; and it says a good deal for Ellen that, brought up as she had been in such a peculiarly sheltered environment, with no sexual knowledge or experience (unlike Mary, she had never indulged in flirtatious petting), she could have been so broadminded about the unfortunate Willy. The letter to Mary continues:

It was stiflingly hot, 90 or more in the cabins and 98 sometimes on deck in the shade, the nights so hot that you poured all the time, I can assure you that it was no joke to nurse him, and Mr Foster has nearly made himself ill, I bore it better than most of the people . . . The Captain hopes we shall get to London Wednesday or Thursday week. The conclusion that Mr Foster, Mr Portal and the other doctors have come to is that Willy is not fit to travel alone, and must either start on a voyage again with a medical attendant, or go and live somewhere quietly with a doctor and his wife. I shall go with him if possible in either case, as anything one can do to make his path a little easier seems only too little. It will be an awful shock to him as he has no idea he is not perfectly responsible for his actions, but in the colonies the punishment for assault on a woman is death and I believe he might easily have come within measurable distance of it. I do not know why Mr Portal changed his mind about our staying out as he heard something he would not tell me. He consulted Lord Carrington, who wrote to Uncle Roger, but I stopped the letter as it seemed to me a most injudicious one. I simply can't express how kind Mr Portal was to me. Lady Carrington and Mr Cartwright were also wonderfully good to me. We went to Melbourne by the overland mail, when we got there Mr Foster's friends who knew tried hard to persuade him not to come with us but I asked

him to as I was afraid, not only of the voyage but of getting to
London again, we are never safe for 24 hours. Mr Foster is going
to get off at Plymouth and see Mr Horsley first, I want something
to be arranged so that we may start away as soon as possible. Mr
Foster is writing to Papa, not that he can do anything. It would
not be safe Willy at a house. I hope you have never breathed a
word of all I have told you. Mr Portal said if he were me he
should tell no one on earth but the doctor, it would always be
against him if it were known. Dr Manning, the mad doctor whom
we saw at Sydney, says Willy must make up his mind to be a
wanderer for a year and a half, it is doubtful if he will ever be
able to rejoin the Army. It seems too hard, Willy does not know.
The Admiral's wife was so kind to me, Mrs Fairfax, but of all the
many who have been good to us, I shall never be able to repay
Mr Foster. He thinks of nothing but how to make things all right
for us and never makes love to me; as he is one of the handsomest
men I have ever seen I can't think why I am not in love with
him. He has been offered £2,000 a year to go and live in Melbourne.

As to life on board, it has, barring all I have told you, been
very passable. There are not many ladies on board and they make
a most absurd fuss of me. I sit next the captain (by invitation)
and there are five men who sit round me all day, they think me
so clever, Heaven knows why. First Mr Foster, of course, then Mr
Hallowes, younger son of a very good Derbyshire family, old
place, deer, etc., etc. He is a nice little man, but getting much too
gone on me. He wants to give me lovely things, which I naturally
won't take, and is always sighing about our future parting, making everyone else laugh. He is coming on though he ought to
have stopped in Cairo. Then Dr Vassie, a Scotchman, consumptive poor man, but very nice and clever. Mr Douglas, another
Scotchman, very good-looking, also ill; he christened me, someone let out, 'Notre Dame de Charité'. Then, about the nicest,
M. Germont, a Frenchman, nephew of Dr Pasteur's, who went to
see about inoculating the rabbits in Australia. He is a great big,
fair haired man and most amusing. He and I keep a public diary
but the other day, when he was sitting up with Willy, at night,
he got very sentimental in it about me and 'un rêve', and he is
coming on to London instead of getting off at Naples to go on

with us, so I had to tell him the diary must not get personal, and he said he knew he was wrong, and apologized and tore it out, which I was (privately) very sorry for, as I wanted to read it again. The whole five are always looking out to do things for me, and they respect me in the funniest way, sort of apologize for talking to me all day, say I must get tired of them etc. We play whist and round games, Dr Vassie and Mr Hallowes sing, and I played my violin till the glue of it melted in the heat, so now I can't. I also hold French class every morning and have developed a talent for caricatures, which is much appreciated, and I sketch a bit, people rather like to have them. I am afraid I certainly shan't marry as you advise. Shall you be in London, I wonder, I will be glad to see you and Harrington and Teddy. The ship has an unpleasant motion, nearly everyone was or felt ill yesterday. I got a fishbone in my throat which stayed there twelve hours and hurt uncommon. Mr Foster was $2\frac{1}{2}$ hours trying to get it out, I was sick several times during the process, it was beastly. I have been having such a curious time, so much anxiety and worry and responsibility, and on the other hand so much help, and the way people have flattered me from Lord Carrington downwards, you wouldn't believe, as if I were doing anything extraordinary. Try and see Lady Loch if you are in London, I love her. There will be such lots of arrangements when we get back to London, oh dear, oh dear. I shall have to stay there anyhow till things are settled up. Mr Foster is very unwell just now, knocked up with looking after Willy. [*Diary*: 'Mr Foster has had another attack and has spit a little blood. I am more sorry than I can say. I believe I had no right to make him come home with us and now he has made himself ill, sitting with Willy. I don't know what to do.'] Hoping to see you soon.

Your affectionate sister,
Ellen

The *Cuzco* touched at Plymouth on June 29th. The previous evening Ellen had taken a long farewell of Mr Foster, sitting on the deck till 11 p.m. He was probably proposing to her for the third time. He left the ship at Plymouth and went straight to London but the rest went on to Tilbury where he met them again – 'he had been spitting blood and looked very ill.'

The parting with the little court was very melancholy. Everyone was very low. We travelled up to London together and sang 'Auld Lang Syne'. We finished the diary, did our last French lesson, I tried in vain to snap my fingers, taught the wink, and then signed the caricatures. They have all been so good to me.

After all this the arrival in London fell very flat. There was difficulty over finding an hotel and the next day's visit to Doctor Horsley did not result, as Ellen had hoped, in immediate arrangements for her future with Willy. He was told to lie up at his rooms in Ryder Street 'and then they are to find a place for him and try to get him to go there'. Mr Foster, as usual, was 'taking all the trouble'. Above all, after the kindness and almost adulation which she had recently encountered, it was a change for Ellen to be faced with the astringent personality of Papa. She went back to North Wales with him, commenting sadly: 'He is the only man I have met I can *not* get on with.'

7

'Tout passe, tout casse, tout lasse'

The next few weeks must have been the most frustrating of Ellen Peel's life. For nine months she had undergone anxiety and sorrow for which nothing in her life had prepared her, and, above all, she had thrown her heart and soul into the attempt to save her brother. All this, not unnaturally, had been accompanied by admiration and appreciation from almost everyone with whom she came in contact. Now she was treated as an importunate and irresponsible child.

It began badly. 'I asked Papa's advice,' she wrote two days after her return, 'and he was most insulting in every way. I will not live here if I can help it.' A week later she wrote out a long account of her position and of her feelings.

Saturday June 29th

I am still here which is the last thing I expected, but Willy does not seem to want me now. I *can't* understand his being allowed to stay in London, and nobody tells me anything or only scraps. It seems hard, I have tried so hard to do for the best, and now everything we had planned seems to be being undone, and I can only look on while things are blurted out to him he need never have known, and he is practically on the loose in London. I suppose I fancied myself too necessary, people were too kind to me while I was away. I fancied I did not believe their compliments, but when you get abused, then is the time to show your vanity. And Willy is so angry with me now, he was so fond of me, though I don't believe he has it in him to be really fond of anybody.

I don't know what or how much they have told him, or how he bore it or anything; I might as well be almost buried, and after living for that for the last 9 months, it does seem a little hard. I was so tired when I got down here and so low that it got on my nerves, but now I am almost apathetic, one can't do more than one can and though one can never say one has done absolutely one's best, still I *have* tried, and that must and shall content me.

My own position is somewhat unpleasant. I had my own money 6 months ago, so I have no right here and they are not on good terms with me. Papa was very fond of me just before he went [he, Mama and Fanny had gone to London] but since then Mama read a letter of mine to Fanny and I am supposed to be corrupting her. And I *can't* get on here. So that outlook isn't rosy, especially as it seems practically for good, you are so walled in here. I might marry. A good many people have liked me since I have been away, and there are two who would marry me now, both like me a thousand times better than I deserve. One [Mr Scrutton] I only knew nine days; he has written to me since I got back and still hopes. I should be ashamed to marry him because I told the other [Mr Foster] I had never loved anybody which was strictly true, and they think so well of me I should hate to lower myself in their eyes. Both would be considered by my people below me in station, and I am snobbish enough to dislike it. The other has known me 6 months nearly. He has given up a great deal for me and though he is a year younger and consumptive I had nearly made up my mind to marry him the day Papa abused me and sneered at me so; but when I told Willy he was madly angry, I don't quite know why, but I suppose it is something he has said about the scrapes he got into abroad. [The pronouns, as frequently happens in Ellen's diaries are mixed, but the sense is clear. Willy may well have disliked Mr Foster who was so frequently given the thankless task of cutting him out with un-desirable ladies, but one feels that the root cause of his anger was jealousy, probably unacknowledged, of Mr Foster's stand-ing with his sister.] So there the matter is at present, though the absurd part is that the man himself had no idea that I even thought of marrying as I refused him 3 times, and I don't know what to do one bit. People were quite ready enough and too ready to like me on the ships and abroad, but in North Wales it is different. I can get on everywhere else but not here. Perhaps I shall be shown a way, I have always been helped hitherto, but I don't deserve it; I have been looking to myself and my own thoughts for guidance, only we never do deserve it. And everybody here makes so little of things which people I knew abroad thought so serious, it makes me nearly light-headed between them. How I wish I had some older woman to go to, to whom I could tell absolutely everything and who would advise me. And if Willy will *only* keep straight and get better I will not mind having my work taken out of my hands just when it was getting easier and will be content not to be wanted any more and thought an officious fool for what I have tried to do. But it is hard that the man who has done so much and given up so much even to his health, he thought his life, for us, should only be snubbed and abused and suspected of heaven knows what by the family. [It is not clear why the Peels were so down on Mr Foster but one imagines that they thought he was making up to Ellen for her money.] Poor Willy. It is natural in him. I must never forget how awfully hard it is and has been for him and how well he has borne it. If he thinks he will have to leave the army nearly everything can be excused to him.

July 2nd

I heard from Mary on Sunday. They all want me to give him up. If I was quite sure of my own mind nothing would make me, but as it is – and Willy is worrying so about it which is bad for him. I have consented to do nothing for the present, and as he doesn't know he will never I suppose ask me again, so there is an end of it. I am not generally superstitious but I told his fortune months ago and I am fulfilling it *myself*, without remembering it till it is too late. They would willingly let me marry the other as a compromise but I won't. I suppose Lord Carrington, Mr Portal, Mr Foster and the doctors were wrong about Willy but – I don't understand it. [Alas they were right. Willy made a partial recovery and in time was supposed to be completely cured, but in 1892 he had to be put under restraint. He had fallen in love with Lady Evelyn Fitzmaurice, daughter of the 5th Marquess of Lansdowne, and believed, almost certainly erroneously, that she was engaged to him. When therefore her marriage to Victor Cavendish, nephew and heir to the Duke of Devonshire, was announced, Willy conceived that she had jilted him and followed her all over London, reproaching her. The Lansdownes and the Cavendishes who knew of his mental state were extremely kind about it, but obviously such a situation could not be allowed to continue, and Willy was relegated to a private home. On Ellen of course fell the task of committing him. In later life she used to say that she had little faith in psychiatrists for she had had great difficulty in convincing the doctors that she was not the patient.]

July 12th

Willy has written to ask me to go to Cowes and Homburg with him. I am so glad. It is better for him and it takes me away from here. They say he is so fond of me, it is such a pleasure to hear it. Only he is staying in London now, but he goes to Glenisland a good deal. He has got on better than we all thought. I wish they had not frightened me so in Sydney. Papa, Mama and Fanny came home yesterday. Fanny looking very nice, I am pleased to see her. I have been having interviews with Papa and Mama which are simply beastly. 'Secret intrigue with my brother's medical adviser', 'double-facedness etc.' The letter [she wrote to Fanny] *was* unlucky, it was enough to make him angry, though I meant no harm. It is the false system, we are afraid of him to his face and laugh at him behind his back, and I have never struggled against it. I am only to consider myself on a visit here, the house is not a hotel, and my return is precarious, but 'Prudence may come in the morning'. I may honestly say that if I hated going I should go for Willy's sake. Mr Horsley does not consider him fit to be left alone. I have made mistakes, but I *have* tried to do for the best, and the united wisdom of Mr Portal, Miss Massey, Mr Foster and myself could see no better way out of it. As to 'secrecy' we consulted only too many, and the difficulties of the position were so many that we could not do what we liked. But I thought, I still think, the advantages of staying in Australia outweighed the others.

Difficulties: Willy's tendency – the law in the colonies – everyone's opinion – Mr Foster's feeling for me – Willy's dread of it.

July 21st

Papa turned round and was very kind and started the Irish plan [presumably that Willy and possibly Ellen should go and live on Uncle Roger's estate in Ireland] and I wrote a letter to Willy that he [Papa] much approved of, but he never answered it and Papa got angry and said I was double-faced and all the rest. So it is 'As you were', though I hope Willy will go to Ireland after Cowes. I wish I could take a house with him for the winter. I am going with him now anyway, the doctor advises it, and I want to. If Papa won't have me back, *tant pis*, but I expect (and hope) he will, as I don't know what I should do. He certainly said he did not object to Cowes, but we had another storm and he denied it, he changes round for any or no reason. The lawn tennis parties here are dull, Mary and Fanny have each their private hopes but I have none. I believe I miss having anyone devoted to me and it is a bore.

Ryder Street [London SW1]

July 27th [1889]

I am here – and I think I wish I wasn't. Willy is *much* better and, I think, quite fit to take care of himself. Hussell says he is ever so much better. It is a great comfort. Everyone was wrong about London and now I feel as if I had wilfully exaggerated things, which I know I didn't, as Willy suspects Mr Foster. He says he *wishes* I had never deceived him and I feel such a beast, though he apologizes in the same breath he still thinks so. And they [the family] will not like my being here and I feel very lonely and as if altogether I had done more harm than good. Is it a lesson against taking one's own way and imagining oneself right?

July 30th

We saw Mr Horsley today. He thinks Willy much better but not fit to live alone and wants me to go with him after his Scotch visits. I will, but don't know where to go between Homburg and Cairo unless they will have me at home. Papa parted from me very kindly so perhaps he will. I did not think he [Dr Horsley] would want me to go on living with him [Willy] but he does, and he says he admires me, which I am sure he needn't. He says we did not exaggerate a bit, that he does not agree with Papa on many points and that he would write to him. He doesn't think we shall be troubled any more with 'Impulses', but there is always a risk. He listened to my heart and says it is all right.

I heard from Mr Foster again, just a line to know where to send my fare. [This is presumably an error for 'his fare', and one imagines that she or the family paid his fare home in return for looking after Willy. Mr Foster, whose Christian name remains shrouded in mystery, is never mentioned in the diary again. As one of Ellen's favourite quotations puts it 'Tout passe, tout casse, tout lasse . . .'] Willy is in good spirits and doesn't much mind my coming to Cairo, it is the time before I am thinking of.

From this point onwards, after the soul-searching of the past few weeks and in an atmosphere of social life, the diary becomes more and more laconic; it is scarcely more than a list of names and engagements. One would appreciate a little more detail. How for instance did she manage about her clothes? She can have had little opportunity and little money for renewing her wardrobe. Did the ubiquitous pink cotton make its appearance again? Presumably she had learnt to cope with her hair, and English chambermaids were probably more obliging than Australian ones over ironing, but it must have been rather daunting to move on to the Squadron lawn and to be presented by Willy to the Prince of Wales ['he was very affable' the diary notes] and such leaders of fashion as the Duchess of Manchester. However such considerations never bothered her much and she seems to have enjoyed herself.

On August 10th they left Cowes and by the 12th they were in Homburg, after a tiresome journey, a bad crossing, and a scene on Frankfurt platform, where 'I was cross and Willy abominably so'. Homburg was at this time the most fashionable of the German spas where the aristocracy of Europe congregated for a month or so to minimize the effects of overeating and drinking. The English, headed by the Prince of Wales, formed the principal contingent, but at first Ellen seems to have felt herself rather lost. 'There seem lots of people here, but I don't know them, which is the loneliest loneliness.' Willy however had a larger acquaintanceship. 'He introduced me to Lady Roseberry, Lady Spencer, the Yarboroughs, Miss Lane Fox, Mr Montgomery and Mr Surtees and I liked it.' She was soon playing tennis (she was good for her sex and times, with a low raking underhand service) with practically everyone, including 'a rather young man, who turned out to be the Duke of Sparta'. Of course it was necessary to take the waters and while doing so she met a long list of people and in the midst of them recorded a 'Mrs Surtees, who is charming'.

Madeleine or Midge Surtees was outstandingly beautiful in an age of beautiful women. She had a lovely oval face, a wealth of bright gold hair, piled on top of her head, deep blue eyes, and, at a time when make-up, except for a little furtively applied *papier poudré*, was taboo, a flawless pink and white complexion. She came by her beauty honestly, for her mother, Miss Herbert, had been one of Rossetti's 'stunners'. More remarkably she had been a successful actressmanageress running her own theatre, on the boards of which Henry Irving made his first London appearance. Somewhere along the line she had married a Mr Crabbe and produced two children, though Midge was more generally thought to be the offspring of a rich north country baronet. After her retirement Miss Herbert was supported by a millionaire, a Mr Maguire. She should have married him, divorcing Edward Crabbe for desertion (he had been missing for almost the requisite period), but unfortunately the inconsiderate husband turned up on the very last permissible day, making the new marriage impossible under English law. The lovers therefore set up house in Switzerland where the divorce laws were easier but Miss Herbert could never be received in English society. It was in church at Nice that Madeleine was seen by a young man who immediately fell in love with her. It was like a fairy story, for Conyers Surtees might have been the model for a Ouida hero. His family was old and aristocratic (the creator of Jorrocks was a distant cousin), he had a fine place in County Durham, he was in the Coldstream Guards, and he was so outstandingly goodlooking that he was known as Beauty Surtees. He had no parents to put obstacles in his way, so that the Prince married Cinderella and they lived happily ever after.

Or did they? In these days they would surely have been divorced, but in those days such a course was almost unthinkable, and they soldiered on through difficult times till, at the end, they became in their seventies as close and devoted a couple as anyone could wish to see.

The main difficulty in the intervening years was that Connie Surtees was like Willy Peel (except that he was perfectly sane) and could never resist the flutter of a woman's petticoat. The list of his conquests was legion. His valet could well have sung Leporello's song. At first Midge was extremely unhappy. Ellen remembered how she would stand at the hotel window in Therapia (Captain Surtees was British military attaché at the Sultan's court) gazing down the street, waiting for her husband to come home, which quite often he did not do. This of course could not last for ever. A remarkably beautiful young woman in her twenties seldom waits indefinitely for a peccant husband. It was not very long before, as Ellen put it, 'things changed'.

At Homburg, however, Midge Surtees was still a recently married woman much in need of a female friend. In many ways she and Ellen made an ideal complement. Midge was not at all intellectual, not even very clever, but she had a great sweetness of nature and an effortless charm of manner. She subdued Ellen's prickles. She built up the self-confidence that had been so eroded in North Wales. She taught Ellen to curb her natural aggressiveness; she made her see that a sharp tongue is not necessarily amusing, that truthfulness need not be confused with rudeness, nor sincerity with outspokenness. In minor ways too she was a lesson to her friend. Ellen was devastatingly untidy; she used to drop everything on the floor and let it lie. It was characteristic of Midge that she uttered no reproaches; she simply followed silently around and picked things up. No amount of scolding would have produced the same effect.

In return Midge gained a friend with the sincerest of affections. Her gay high spirits made her a delightful companion. Moreover although she never bored Connie she never flirted with him; in fact she once told him that she thought she was the only woman he had ever met whom he had not attempted to seduce!

The two women took to each other immediately. It was less than a week after their first meeting that Mrs Surtees asked Ellen to come back with them to Constantinople. Ellen thought this a 'lovely plan', and adhered to it, even though Papa, whose bark was often worse than his bite, wrote saying that he would have her back. The only difficulty was Willy. The Prince himself spoke to her saying that he did not think Willy ought to be left alone. This was all very well but Willy was under no kind of restraint. Ellen suggested the Prince might speak directly to Willy and she consulted the Surteeses and Hussell: 'they all think he oughtn't to be left by himself, but don't see how to manage it.' It was no good. She tried her best; she even prevented Willy being called on the morning of his departure for England, 'but all no use, he went.' On August 30th she wrote: 'My birthday. I did not expect to be here with Willy gone, and I have failed, and I think I might have done better, selfishness as usual in the way.' She had little need to reproach herself on that score, and it is something of a pleasure to find that after so much care and anxiety the next three months were to be delightful and carefree and fun.

She set off on August 31st in a railway carriage smothered in flowers, mostly, she says, on account of Mrs Surtees. The fourth member of the party was Maurice Fremantle, a brother officer of Connie Surtees, with whom Ellen, who was three years his senior, was soon on the most excellent brotherly terms. Their relationship was essentially a modern one somewhat incomprehensible to Victorian society. 'They always put him down to Mrs Surtees or me, the Prince says he is in love with her, at Therapia they said he was engaged to me and anything more improbable than either is yet to be found.' Ellen described him as 'a funny boy, perfectly charming, the most unflirtatious person I ever saw. He and I quarrel and make up and he helps us pack and mend our clothes and anything that comes handy.'

Mr Fremantle also took charge of Ellen's diamonds which hitherto she had mostly carried about in her pocket (on one occasion, during a game of tennis, pulling out her handkerchief and scattering a shower of diamond stars on the court). On the journey from Homburg to Constantinople the two of them generally occupied adjoining rooms and carried on cheerful conversation while dressing; it was no wonder that they were usually taken for husband and wife, though Ellen writes that she once got annoyed with Mr Fremantle for encouraging the waiters to call her 'madam'. On the whole however it was a wonderfully harmonious quartet and any disagreements ended in ragging or, as the Victorians termed it, 'bear-fighting – the oddest pastime for that era, involving a good deal of personal contact, pushing and shoving, and becoming quite rough.

Saturday September 14th

Got to Sofia about 12 and went to the Grand Hotel de Bulgarie and cleaned ourselves. The English Consul, Mr O'Connor, came and took us for a drive. Capt. Surtees collected information and we collected flowers near the sulphur baths. Mr O'Connor was very amusing and told us about the Bulgarian ladies, he was much shocked about Busvine's habits, seems so ridiculous. [Busvine was the smart tailor for riding clothes. This probably refers to the safety habits, which had just superseded the long flowing skirts of an earlier date.]

Sunday September 15th

The telegram came so we started. Mr O'Connor much disappointed by not taking me out riding in my Busvine's habit. They came to see us off, I like her very much, but she has rather a bad time of it, ill, with no one to look after her and no chloroform when she had a baby. We went to Bellover in a common carriage and then got into a special which Baron Hirsch had given the Surteeses, very comfortable. [Ellen's mother had followed the same route forty-five years earlier, but she had travelled by bullock cart and slept on the floor.] We read the lessons first, I read one out loud to Capt. Surtees and then played cards. Slept pretty comfortably but not very, and got to Constantinople about eight o'clock, (bearfought with pins), it looked more Eastern than I expected and not quite so many English people. We had a small breakfast of Turkish Delight and grapes and came on here [Therapia] by steamer. I was never more tired in my life, being unwell. We unpacked, everyone wondered at the amount in my box, and then we had tea, letters, one for Mrs S. from Willy, Mr Horsley has sent him out here by the 15th to join me, I am much relieved, and I daresay Cairo will be nice, but I am sorry to leave Mrs Surtees and the others, and it is a responsibility and lonely work. I suppose it will be easier now though. Mrs Surtees found a bug in her bed, which put us out very much as we did think this was a clean place. [They stayed on however and eventually became very fond of the Hotel d'Angleterre, more generally known as Petala's, from the name of the proprietress. It appeared to harbour a strange ramshackle collecton of polyglots: one, whom they nicknamed 'the Countess', took a violent fancy to Mr Fremantle, only dissipated when on her asking him to unlace her stays he tied the laces to the banisters.] Ellen's diary entry for September 15th concluded 'Went out in two caiques on the Bosphorus, sounds interesting and wasn't.'

Ellen Palmer's diary of 1855 had ended with almost the same words: 'We all went in caiques to the Sweet Waters of Europe,' and the Sublime Porte itself had changed very little however since 1855.

It was still under the despotic control of a Sultan, now Abdul Hamid, Abdul the Damned. On the rare occasions when he ventured forth from the safety of his seraglio Ellen could observe him surrounded by armed troops, his upright figure supported it was said by a steel corselet, and his nervous black eyes roving from side to side.

Friday September 20th

Went to Constantinople to see the Salamnik, a magnificent sight, and review of the troops afterwards. We had a good view of the Sultan. The Zouaves are very smart, the whole thing, fezes, flags, horses, mosques, profusion gold and glitter was like the stage. Black coffee, bad, and teal that had never seen the sea. Got back late and very hungry.

One or two more Turkish visits are recorded in the diary, though for some reason it does not mention the occasion when she and the Surteeses went, on a very hot night, to dine with the Sultan's brother-in-law. They went in high hopes, for he was supposed to have the best cook in Turkey, but alas! as a compliment to their nationality they were regaled with roast beef and plum pudding, while the private band played 'God Save the Queen' without ceasing.

Sunday September 22nd

Went to Constantinople quite early to see the Dvinish Pasha. He and his two sons received us most affably, one who had married the Sultan's daughter interpreted. He [the Pasha] was a nice old man, exchanged cigarettes with us, and presented the Surteeses with two donkeys, two ponies, a picture and a foal. [What did they do with this assorted livestock?] We spilt our coffee and felt rather fools, then went out to see his harem, only two ladies, his wife and Ali Bey's mother. Afterwards we saw the horses, and Ali Bey who was most amusing, offered me his horse, said I was a *'demoiselle gaie'*, regretted not being able to marry a European etc. [Ellen was still very plump and she pleased Turkish taste much more than the beautiful Mrs Surtees.] I never realized before what a despotic country it is, spies everywhere, you have to report even your lunch parties.

Friday September 27th

Mrs Surtees and I went to a harem, we were rather bored, the Ministre de la Marine's harem. They asked me if I could not get a husband or if I did not want one. It must be an awful life like an imprisoned animal. Mrs Surtees and I got photographed in yash-maks, we blacked our eyes, and then we went to see the dancing dervishes, a curious but interesting sight.

Life among the Turks however impinged very little on that of the foreign community, riding, playing tennis and flirting on the shores of the Bosphorus. Ellen resumed her long diary letters to Mary.

October 10th 1889

Dearest Mary,

I forget if I have written to you since I got your letter and Fanny's enclosed one, very nice long ones, I was so pleased to get them. The other day when I was riding with Mr Lowther [Gerard Lowther, nephew of the 3rd Earl of Lonsdale, one of the secre-taries at the Embassy in Constantinople] I heard the dogs bay in the woods just like the hounds at Wynnstay, and it made me feel as homesick as possible for a few minutes. Now Teddy has gone and all [Teddy had gone into the Army and been sent abroad] it has broken up our old party, I don't suppose we shall ever be so jolly again quite. I am writing this because Mr Fremantle and I have quarrelled at picquet, because I wanted him to pick up some cards and he wouldn't, so we have separated in dudgeon. We have dined out several times, generally five from the hotel which gave a certain sameness about it. At the ambassador's [Sir Wil-liam White's] I was rather a success as he talked to me at dinner and afterwards took me to a secluded seat, and had been praising me up to the secretaries since, much to their amusement as he doesn't generally do it. He says I am so nice and clever. He is rather a wicked old man and rather vulgar, but he is an ambassa-dor 'et c'est toujours quelqu'chose'. Lord Zouche has gone. Mrs Surtees had a decided penchant for him herself, she tried to bring it on and used to talk to him about me. He said of his own accord that I was so bright it made such a difference when I came into the room, and we used to gaze at each other, but never got any further. His last evening we were both very well disposed for a talk but alas! two *old married* men, who are a precious sight too fond of me grappled hold, and when I had dodged them and got into a nice corner with him, if one of them didn't lumber up and make a third on the sofa, the fool! I went to bed in a rage, but the sad part of the story is this, that since his departure we hear that he only came here because there was a scandal about Lady Cadogan [Beatrix, daughter of the Earl of Craven and wife of 5th Earl Cadogan; what the scandal can have been it is impossible to say] which has put us quite off him. [Lord Zouche however would never 'have done', as the phrase used to be. The diary records him as 'getting rather shocked by our putting a fish in Mr Fremantle's bed'.]

My flirtation with Mr Lowther is very quiet and rather slow, he comes and fetches me for lawn tennis etc., but don't get much further. My lawn tennis is immensely admired here and I play a very correct game of whist. The day before yesterday I went for a riding picnic which was rather fun, but whenever I was riding with anyone at all fascinating someone else came up, in fact you might as well try to flirt in an oyster barrel as here. One old man in particular, General Blunt, is such a marplot, that Mrs Surtees believes he is paid to interrupt us. I have been asking her to teach me to flirt properly, but she says she doesn't know how and that I get on very well with men, but I cannot disguise from myself that I don't know how to bring people on, and yet one ought with all the practice that Sav gave us, he was like a wily old salmon.

Later in the day

I have been having awful fun, I went late to the tennis, and having had three sets with Mr Jolliffe, against Mr Fremantle and another, Mr Lowther appeared and offered to play me a single (he is the champion of Turkey) and I played two with him and he said he had come on purpose to see me and not finding me had gone away again which is the first pretty thing he has ever said to me.

Mrs Surtees came in very angry, she had been out to tea and they tell her that his old love is furiously jealous of me, which made her so angry that she intends to make her hair stand on end. We are going out a riding party tomorrow (he has offered to take me alone and I shall accept), we [Mrs Surtees and herself]

mean to have some fun, but if he don't do his part I shall be very
angry now. Sir Edgar Vincent [later Lord D'Abernon] is coming
today. Mrs Surtees says he is the most fascinating man alive and
an awful flirt, so I am expecting to see him much smit with her.

Do you hear anything of Willy? I have become nervous about
him these last days, I don't know why.

Love to all,

Your affectionate sister,
Ellen

October 23rd

Dearest Mary,

Thursday

I went for a ride with Mr Lowther in the afternoon, it was
very amusing, but he isn't a bit in love with me though the others
think he is. We had a delicious ride over the heather, he came
back to tea and they asked him to stop to dinner, and he stayed
and played picquet with me all the evening. He is awfully amusing and nice and tells me his things. He is awfully conceited and I
laugh at him like anything which he doesn't mind a bit.

Friday

We dined at the Embassy. I sat next Sir Edgar Vincent, who is
supposed to be one of the greatest lady killers out, and an old
admirer of Mrs Surtees's, says the rudest things that come into his
head, he said he knew I was very bad tempered but very good-
natured, he had heard I was an immense genius, said he had
watched me at the hotel, he discussed Mrs Surtees's personal
appearance. After dinner Mrs Surtees and he ought to have con-
glomerated, but she was sitting by the ambassador and he came to
me (we had been getting on very well) and invited me to go into
the card-room with him, and when the secretaries came in there
we were and, there not being much choice, he stuck to me the
whole of the evening. That would have been very amusing (he
is an awful flirt) but other men kept joining, there are so few
women, and I couldn't even do that [flirt] but it looked like it
and Mr Lowther got as sulky as a bear and wouldn't speak to me
when he might. Sir Edgar doesn't believe in love a bit, he is, I

suppose, really more of a married woman's flirt than anything else, and he is so accustomed to women falling in love with him that he rather resents it if they don't.

Sunday

The Surteeses went to Constantinople, but I stayed till Monday with Mrs Blunt, a dear old lady. I went to Holy Communion and warbled in the choir at 11 o'clock, walked home with Sir Edgar, but saw nothing of Mr Lowther who was in attendance on Ly. White. After lunch I got a note from Mr Lowther, rather to my delight, to know if I would ride or what I should like to do. I promptly threw over an engagement with Dr Macnamara and rode. We had a lovely ride, flirting enough to be amusing and nothing more. How conceited men are! I can't repeat some of the things he told me but it is really amazing. We met Sir William Gordon Cumming and Major Herbert, whom I know, riding with Col. Trotter. Sir William took me for you and began talking to me, but I have heard such dreadful things of him that I declined to scrape acquaintance. [It is interesting that Sir William's reputation should already have been so bad, for it was more than a year before the notorious Tranby Croft scandal when he was accused of cheating at baccarat.] He told Mrs Surtees he knew you quite well.

In the evening we went to a party at the Embassy. Sir William White took me by the arm and conducted me to an ottoman, which, if a bore, impressed other people, he is very fond of me. Then Sir Edgar Vincent asked me again to come into the card-room with him (he said he couldn't get anyone to sit down) which has nice dark corners, and we were getting on beautifully when another man had the stupidity to join us. After that being the last evening, all my friends came, Mr Jolliffe, Mr Tower, Col. Trotter, Mr Harding, Mr Lowther. I forgot to say I got a note from Mr Lowther at dinner to play a small picquet debt and to ask for my photograph. We did not get left alone, at last Mr Hardinge [afterwards Lord Hardinge of Penshurst] having persistently made a third to Sir Edgar and Mr Lowther, I sent him away, and then we had our last good-byes. I told him of the few nice things he had said to me, he said he couldn't express his feelings when he felt (all half in fun), we promised an exchange of photographs, squeezed hands and – parted, and I regret to say Sir William told Mrs Surtees I looked very down.

We had our fortunes told by a gipsy the other day. She told Mrs Surtees a secret of hers that she couldn't possibly have known, most curious. [The secret was that Mrs Surtees was *enceinte*. It must however have been a false alarm or a miscarriage must have supervened – the eldest Surtees child was not born till thirteen months later.] Mine was nothing peculiar. She said I was fond of sleep and *'bonne pour tout le monde, homme et femmes'*, and that I had an affair *'qui balancait'* but would come right (not so) but we could only speak to her through an interpreter and I asked no further. She burnt away the evil with hot coals from Mrs Surtees and put an egg in her bosom to purge her, which she threw away. I am so tired of writing. Mind you don't read any more of my letter to Mama than is good for her, I am rather afraid you do.

Much love,

Your affec. sister,
Ellen

8

'Their conversation is unrepeatable'

It is an interesting sidelight on Victorian society, amply borne out by many incidents in Trollope's novels, that men could flatter, hint and imply devotion, besides taking as many physical privileges, such as hand squeezing and even kissing, as the girls would allow them without feeling themselves bound in the smallest degree. It seems that not until the five plain words 'Will you be my wife?' were spoken was anything regarded as the least serious. Once the fatal compact was made however, it was looked on as virtually unbreakable.

Gerard Lowther's influence does not seem to have lasted long. In her next letter to Mary Ellen wrote: 'We are getting along very nicely here. One sees so many things and people, men especially, that by the time you answer my letters I have nearly forgotten the ones you allude to, they are always changing.' 'Here' was Athens, to which the Surtees party had migrated at the end of October in order to attend the wedding of the Duke of Sparta, eldest son of the King of the Hellenes (Ellen had played tennis with him at Homburg), and Princess Sophie, the daughter of the widowed Princess Frederick of Prussia. Athens was chock-a-block with royalties and their suites, including the Prince of Wales, who arrived in the Royal yacht the *Osborne*, with her escort vessel the *Surprise*. The *Osborne* was commanded by Captain the Hon. Hedworth Lambton (afterwards Hedworth Meux), a younger son of the Earl of Durham, and the *Surprise* by Captain the Hon. Maurice Bourke, a brother of the Earl of Mayo. The two Captains were very soon on friendly teasing terms with Midge and Ellen, calling on them in the evenings and telling them it was 'indecorous' to throw things into the street.

The young women also saw a good deal of the Prince. He seems to have been very 'affable', to use one of Ellen's favourite words. She tells Mary that they 'met him on the Acropolis, and

... he came here to call on Mrs Surtees and got us all asked to meet him at the Monsons' [British Embassy] yesterday. I don't mind talking to him a bit now, he is just like anyone else, only you have to stick 'Sir' in every sentence and I find great difficulty in bringing it in naturally, and you feel everyone is listening to what he says to you. He called me up yesterday and talked to me for some time, but of course he likes talking to Mrs Surtees better than anyone, he is awfully fond of her, but quite friendly, he doesn't flirt with her one bit. He wants to know everything, who we flirted with at Therapia, he was of opinion that Mr Lowther would do very well for me, and that his father ought to be very pleased. He asked Mrs Surtees if she was a success at Therapia to which she replied that all the young men went out riding with me, which was a frightful libel, and then he asked if I was fond of flirting, he wants to know everything.

I suppose you read Mama's letter so I won't describe the wedding. [The diary records the brief and rather crushing comment: 'The bride looked very pretty for her.] It is most annoying the Prince won't be here for the ball, not that I think he would have been much use to me, but he said that Col. Clarke would introduce people to us. Willy arrives on Tuesday I hope.

All this intercourse with the *beau monde* did not entirely divert Ellen's mind from her sisters' affairs. She wrote to Mary on October 30th:

Thank you so much for your letters, I have got them all, I am so pleased to get them, though the last made me very angry. I think Papa ought to be kicked. I am so glad you are going to Kenure [Uncle Roger's estate in county Dublin], it *ought* to come off then, mind it does. Sav's note amused me highly, he has got on since the old days. I am much disappointed about four figures, for after your letter I had been daily expecting to hear it was all settled. I think he *must* mean something or if he don't he ought to be hung. Does Harrington mind his going away?

Willy arrived yesterday, he was very well, I was so pleased to see him again and he to see me. [Diary: 'Willy arrived after dinner, very cheerful and very nice, but I don't see all that improvement in him I wish, he still laughs that dreadful laugh. I am so pleased to see him again, and so is he to see me. They all call me "Peelings" or "Peel minor" now.']

We went to the ball last night. Such a ball! People squashed so tight except in a space about 20ft. square, railed off for the royalties. No refreshments except supper, and that a perfect beargarden, men fighting for the champagne and everyone sticking their dirty forks into the dishes. No servants' ball in England would have been so disorderly. (Mrs. S. actually brought back a bug in her dress.) One of the secretaries tried to smuggle me into the diplomatic supper room, but alas! all the places were marked and we had to beat a hasty and undignified retreat.

We went to the *Osborne* and *Surprise* and saw the Prince off. Capt. Bourke and Capt. Lambton were very nice but their conversation isn't improving by any means. [*Diary:* 'Went to the *Osborne* and *Surprise*. Their conversation sometimes is unrepeatable and I never know what to do under the circumstances, they were dreadful in the Prince's cabin.'] We have seen a good deal of them. We had a dreadful bear fight the other day, rather reminded me of our old Kenure days. [*Diary:* 'We bearfought in the evening too much till we got a little cross, locking doors etc.']

Love to everyone,

Your affectionate sister,

Ellen

The dreary ball was followed by a visit to the Peloponnese. As usual Mary was not bothered by any descriptions of scenery or excursions into Greek history.

I told Mama about our voyage to Nauplia and Agamemnon's tomb and the citadel of old Corinth and all the rest of it, you probably heard. Travelling here ain't all beer and skittles not by no means. The smells at Nauplia were so bad that Mrs Surtees had to go out to be sick in the middle of dinner, the food is mostly cooked with buffalo butter, and what *that* is you have no idea till you try, and it is advisable to have an exhaustive hunt in your bed before you go to rest. Next week we mean to go to Corfu, across Thessaly, they say it is a *very* rough journey, we are to have an escort for fear of brigands, but it excites the people here very much, and they say Mrs Surtees and I oughtn't to go. Willy is going by sea. He wanted to go straight to Cairo from here, but

Mrs Surtees persuaded him to come. I shall hate to part, we have such fun sometimes.

Before the perilous journey across Albania there was a last week in Athens which proved highly enjoyable. The Surteeses naturally moved a good deal in diplomatic society and they were given a farewell dinner at the Legation. Dinner itself was not very amusing. Ellen sat between 'old Sir Edmond' (the British Minister) 'and Colonel Hall, who is very clever and always talks like a book, and a very dry one.' After dinner conversation, however, was more rewarding:

> Mr Haggard nearly gave me a fit. He is married, but a great old flirt, and we were sitting on a sofa together and he was telilng me that he had never found *the* woman etc., etc. 'Oh Mr Haggard,' I said, as innocently as I could, 'but you're married.' 'Does a man cease to be a man,' he said indignantly, 'because he is married? May a man not think, not feel? May a poor man at least,' softening, 'not have his recollections?' He was looking so sentimental at this point that I couldn't help it, I exploded and laughed till the tears came into my eyes. He was very good about it and laughed too, I thought I should have died, but he didn't go on with his sentiment. Afterwards I talked to Mr Des Graz, who is rather what we used to call Fencock, a 'universal'. He also must begin about his 'ideal', and what a good husband he should make, and all quite seriously, he don't understand chaff. I think diplomats are a little cracked.
>
> When there is nothing else to do Mr Fremantle and I either play picquet or dominoes or go for a walk. He is such a funny boy, perfectly charming, the most unflirtatious person I ever saw, I think he is so used to being fallen in love with, they make eyes at him everywhere, he is so good-looking. He and I quarrel and make up and he helps us pack and mend our clothes or anything that comes handy. He is very poor, poor boy, and has hard work to live on his allowance.

More exciting however than diplomatic society or the oddly modern comradeship with Mr Fremantle was the return of the Prince of Wales, who brought with him the two naval captains of the *Osborne* and the *Surprise*. Of the men they met in Athens, Ellen told Mary, 'far the most interesting is Captain Bourke of the *Surprise*, Mrs Surtees and I squabble over him!' He seems to have distributed his favours fairly evenly. When they went to luncheon on board the *Surprise* and Mrs Surtees asked him for a photograph, Ellen was touched and pleased that he offered her one too.

Captain Lambton made no secret of his preference for Mrs Surtees. He organized an expedition to the Acropolis by moonlight, one of the great diversions of Athens society. 'It is awfully funny,' Ellen told her sister, 'you see couples you know (Mr Haggard was half a couple), couples who would prefer not to be seen, couples who stay in the shadows etc.' On this occasion Captain Lambton's plans did not work out as he had hoped.

November 8th

The Acropolis is lovely, but our attention was distracted at the entrance by meeting the Prince with Prince George of Greece and Prince Waldemar of Denmark who he introduced to us, and then walked up with Mrs Surtees, much to Captain Lambton's indignation who had meant to do it himself. He is a most *owdacious* flirt and, I think, would much like to flirt with her. I expect he would with anyone pretty, or anyone else if the pretty people were unobtainable. There is a big ruin, the Parthenon, there with a dark inside stair, he invited me to come with him, Mrs S. being unobtainable, it would have been fun, but unluckily I did not hear. Willy did not come, his toe is inclined to gather again, the Prince asked me where he was and whether he was in a prison cell, the only place, he thought, where he would keep quiet.

Captain Lambton was not to be so easily deflected. He came to tea the next day and, Ellen wrote in her diary, 'they' (presumably the other guests) 'would not go but we sat in a circle till I said something awful and they' (this time certainly Captain Lambton and Mrs Surtees) 'went out on the balcony and had a – conversation. He admires her very much. She *says* he says I am charming and like an American. We played vingt-et-un in the evening. Capt. Lambton came back but he didn't get any opportunity of speaking to her.'

Midge Surtees had any number of admirers during her long life,

mostly among the smartest members of the Prince of Wales's set.*
Ellen however always maintained, and she should have known,
that Hedworth Lambton was Midge's *amant du coeur*, a relationship that must have begun during this visit to Athens. Perhaps
Connie noticed something, for the next day Ellen records that the
Surteeses had a row. Discreetly she adds no details. To aggravate
matters, Willy, with one of his periodical fits of decorum as far as
his sister was concerned, 'objected to my working in Mr Fremantle's
bedroom.' But the clouds rolled away and three days later they
started on their journey. Willy prudently decided to go by sea, but
the other four went overland by way of Thessaly and Southern
Albania to Corfu. It was quite a perilous enterprise; no foreign
woman and very few foreign men had crossed that way. The moun-
tains were infested by brigands and the party was accompanied by
a military escort. As usual Ellen leaves accounts of natural beauties
and past history for Mama; Mary is simply told that it is 'the finest
scenery in the world'. Nor does the diary amplify much. From it
one gains the impression that the journey while it lasted was uncomfortable, dangerous and boring, and that the travellers enjoyed
it enormously.

Their escort through Thessaly consisted of Albanian troops, an
officer and three exceedingly good-looking corporals. They visited
the fourteenth-century monastery of Meteora, built as a refuge for
hermits among towering, almost perpendicular, rocks. The men of
the party were pulled up by ropes and baskets; the two ladies were
not, of course, allowed to participate, but the Father Superior, a
bibulous and friendly old gentleman, came down and spent a con-
vivial evening with them. At the Turkish frontier (Albania at that
time was a Turkish possession) they exchanged their handsome

---

* The one who bulked largest in her life (though quite possibly was never her
lover) was the popular Jack Brabazon, known throughout society as 'Bwab'. After
one meeting with Midge in a railway carriage, he became an integral part of her
life. The Prince of Wales himself complained that Bwab would never accept an
invitation unless he was quite sure that Mrs Surtees did not want him. He had been
forced, through extravagance, to transfer out of the Guards into a line regiment,
and in this connexion made the celebrated *mot* which finally found its way into
Punch: 'Can't wemember what they are called, but you get to them by changing
at Weading and they have gween on their cuffs.' Consistently inexpert at recog-
nizing people, he once thought he saw an unusually pretty kennelmaid crossing
the stable yard at Sandringham. He stole up behind her, clipped her round the
waist and gave her a smacking kiss. Only then did he realize that it was his hostess,
the Princess of Wales, who sensibly decided the Prince should not hear of it.

corporals for forty-one Turkish soldiers. It was on the frontier that Ellen made her entry into the little town of San Stefano, on a Turkish horse, riding sideways on a man's saddle – no mean test of horsemanship. 'I was never in such a funk in my life, sideways on this thing, going down a sort of precipice over loose stones.'

They went through all the usual experiences of travelling in Balkan or Middle Eastern countries. 'Sometimes we slept in private houses, the women generally in the national costume, they receive you with a tray of jam and little glasses of liqueur, very good, only you're expected to drink them all day long. All the evening we used to sit solemnly and express ourselves by pantomime.' At Baldour Khan they all had to sleep in one room and 'Mr Fremantle mended my dress in his pyjamas in the firelight.' At Lugos Khan there were two rooms, and Ellen's bed collapsed to reveal the remains of the courier's dinner, which he had thriftily placed inside it. At Prevesa they were returning to civilization and found an English and an Italian consul, spring beds, and early morning tea. A day later they slept on board the Austrian Lloyd steamer which was to take them to Corfu.

At Corfu they re-encountered Willy, 'in excellent spirits', and Ellen thought that he 'seemed really better'. Alas it was not long before the old trouble cropped up again.

Monday December 2nd
    Capt. Surtees told me that Willy had been writing to the manager's wife, there is also a chambermaid, someone at the opera to whom he wrote a love letter and who stuck it up, the prima donna, to whom he sent a bouquet and who returned it. I did think it was all right now. He spoke to Willy, he is very kind about it.

Tuesday
    Willy woke up with a cold and wants to go away. I consulted the Surtees in bed about it, who don't think I ought to go with him, he [Capt. Surtees] nearly wrote to Papa, but I shall.

The next day the men of the party decided to go on a shooting expedition in Albania. Ellen, who 'had the blues', wanted to go with them but the yacht was too small so she stayed behind with Mrs Surtees.

Thursday

We went to see them off, came back, poked about the town, slept in the same room, had our nice little breakfasts together and a good gossip. Midge told me a lot about Willy, also a thrilling anecdote of Lady Walter Campbell, Mr Bonham, Mr Hawtrey, the Dss. of Leinster etc.

Monday December 9th

They arrived quite early, having shot nothing, but apparently enjoyed themselves. We went for a long drive and bearfought frightfully, they pulled me on to their knees and took off my boots I am ashamed to say.

Four days later the little party boarded an Austrian Lloyd steamer. The Surteeses and Maurice Fremantle got off at Brindisi en route for home, and the Peels went on to Cairo.

I don't think I ever felt more desolate than when they went away in a shore boat in the half light at four o'clock with a cold morning and a misty moon. They *have* been nice to me. I feel perfectly lost without her. He is nearly as nice, and Mr Fremantle, only he is so perfectly indifferent to me which would take off from the charms of an archangel.

9

'I - very much against my will - was married'

It was not long before Ellen had to face up once more to the responsibilities of her lonely position. During all their time in Greece Connie Surtees had looked after Willy, allowing Ellen to enjoy her holiday. Now the onerous task began again.

Wednesday December 18th
    The Captain sent for me to complain of Willy, he tried four times to get into a lady's cabin and they are all in a fright.

For the first time Ellen was forced to speak to Willy herself about his behaviour. Up to now they had tacitly avoided discussing his lapses, and the fact that she was able to put the situation into words shows a change of attitude. She was no longer the provincial younger sister, in spite of everything still rather in awe of, and dazzled by, her big brother. She now had no intermediary like Mr Foster or Captain Surtees and she tackled the problem head on. 'He has promised never to do it again,' she wrote, 'but it is a bad beginning.' Her direct intervention seems to have had a good effect, for during the whole three months they were in Egypt Willy gave no further trouble and when they left his doctor wrote to her as follows: 'I am happy to be able to tell you that your brother leaves Cairo improved in every respect, I may almost say a new man. This is almost entirely owing to your care of him, and to the moral influence you have exercised over him.'
    Another moral influence, possibly an unconscious one, may have been that of Colonel Kitchener. During his service in Egypt Willy had been Kitchener's ADC, and obviously retained a great respect for him. He had talked a great deal about him to Ellen, and he must have been pleased when the great man himself came to meet them at the station at Cairo.
    Kitchener was just beginning to rise in his meteoric career. A year previously he had led his Sudanese brigade in a spirited and

victorious engagement at Suakim. In January 1889 he had returned to Cairo as Adjutant General, and in August of the same year he had commanded the cavalry at the British victory of Toski. He was unpopular in Cairo and with his brother officers but there was no doubt that he was a coming man. He was also exceedingly good-looking, 'tall and spare with the most wonderful piercing blue eyes, set very far apart.' Now he began to pay marked attention to Ellen Peel.

It is here that, most aggravatingly, the correspondence with Mary ceases. We can well spare the descriptions of the Nile and the Pyramids which doubtless went to Mama; but it would be most interesting to have an uninhibited and truthful account of Colonel Kitchener's courtship. The diary is again hardly more than a list of engagements. All we can gather is the following. The day after the Peels arrived in Cairo Kitchener asked them to tea, and 'he was very nice and gave me some roses'. He got them an invitation to the Grenfells' dance and Ellen danced with him. Two days later he came to tea at their hotel and offered her his pony to ride. During the next fortnight she saw him nearly every day. She walked about and had tea with him at the races, she rode home with him from the polo ground, she met him at a children's party. On January 5th she 'put Col. Kitchener off and he can't come tomorrow, most annoying' but he called the same evening and went with her to an evening party. On the 7th 'Col. Kitchener came to dinner, we played picquet afterwards and he stayed quite late.' On January 9th Colonel Kitchener and Ellen, Major Maxwell and Miss Bonynge rode out to a paper chase together. 'Col. Kitchener and I rode together all the time and home, and I think the others did too.'

Louise Bonynge was Ellen's principal girl friend in Cairo. She in no way took the place of Midge Surtees, but she was gay and attractive and full of gossip. Her father was an American who had made a fortune out of the Civil War. He was always known as 'old Bonynge', and appears to have been something of a lecher and something of a joke. Very early in their acquaintance Ellen wrote 'I drove to the racecourse with Mr Bonynge, who made me the most extraordinary confidences in every way. I think he must be cracky. He came to my room in the evening and made an extraordinary fool of himself . . . I was angry.' Louise Bonynge was more attractive than her father. She was slender, with bright red hair and enormous eyes. She used to sing slightly improper little French songs to the guitar, which was found extremely fetching. She was a great flirt, but her sights were probably set on Major Maxwell, always known as 'Conky', and after a good few vicissitudes she finally married him. He became General Sir John Maxwell, and greatly added to our troubles in Ireland, by his severity after the Easter Rising. He would probably not have been well advised by his wife. When someone trod on her toe in a Cairo tram she retaliated by stamping on his with all the force of a four-inch heel. In old age she remained very thin, plastered with make-up, smelling almost overpoweringly of scent, and her red hair flamboyantly dyed. She always maintained that Colonel Kitchener had proposed to Ellen.

He never did, but he certainly was what the Victorians called 'very attentive'. He and Ellen and Miss Bonynge and Major Maxwell made up their 'usual four' on more than one occasion. On one such the diary records that a Mrs Settle remarked, possibly a trifle sourly, that Ellen 'seemed to be having a good time', and the diarist added in brackets, 'So I was.' But the good time came to an end. There was a dance which proved to be 'a most disappointing evening in every way, it was as much as I could do to look pleasant, and couldn't sleep after it, it reminded me of the days of my youth.' It must have been this evening, though the diary does not say so, that she went to bed in tears. Mingled with her chagrin however there was a certain elation. It had come to her, now she knew what it was like. All the pangs undergone by Mary and Fanny and Midge and Louise and Lily Piercy were now hers. At last, at last, she was really and truly in love. The next morning she could not persuade herself that she cared a button.

'Recovered my spirits, especially after a gossip with Louise.' Louise held the comforting theory that Colonel Kitchener had only been so unsatisfactory because a certain Madame d'Aubigny had just returned to Cairo and that she had been his mistress. He did not like to flaunt his new love in the face of the old. Whether or not there was any truth in this theory, which seems impossible, Colonel Kitchener had certainly cooled off. The affair dragged on a little. Ellen once even took a charm with her when she dined with him, 'but had no opportunity of using it.' She cannot have tried very hard, for their host asked her and Willy to stay on 'but I wouldn't, I can't think why.' At the Khedive's ball, although she danced nearly all the time with him and with a Captain Graham, it was disappointing: 'He was dull or sleepy or bored I think,' and when, a week later, he came to tea and said that he could not ride with her, she reverted to the slang of her youth and 'had a compulsory funeral'.

She was not heartbroken. During the final fortnight of ons and offs with Colonel Kitchener another dark horse had been coming up on the rails. Captain Henry Graham of the 20th Hussars had been her other partner at the Khedive's ball and after that she saw a good deal of him. He came to tea, he came to play tennis and stayed to lunch, and, at Lady Baring's ball, where Ellen danced only once with Colonel Kitchener she 'sat out several dances with Captain Graham and talked of all sorts of subjects.'

Henry Graham was not such a striking personality as Colonel Kitchener, but he was probably easier to get on with. He was a good-looking, heavily built man (his brother officers called him 'Jumbo'), with a sweeping cavalry moustache. His father had started the firm of Graham and Nicholson, which made gin, but after a comfortable fortune had been amassed William Graham was persuaded by his sons to sell out, on the grounds that trade was low (the Nicholsons stayed in and became very much richer). William must have been something of a character. He kept a very successful racing stable* but his wife disapproved of racing, so for many years he ran it under an assumed name. When he won the Ascot Gold Cup he refused to be presented to the Prince of Wales as was customary, because the Grahams were Jacobites and would never recognize the House of Hanover.

By 1890, however, old Graham was dead, the gin was comfortably forgotten, and Henry, in a crack regiment with a reputed £10,000 a year (it was really only £2,000) was regarded, as Ellen used to say, in an oddly dated little phrase, as 'the parti of Cairo'. He had been in love with Lady Evelyn Murray, the daughter of Lord Dunmore, but she, greatly to her mother's annoyance, preferred a less eligible brother officer, Captain Beech. It did not take Captain Graham long to change his allegiance. On January 6th Ellen wrote 'I had a long talk with Captain Graham, he is I *think* a little

* His filly Formosa won the five Classics.

gone on Lady Evelyn, he was so angry at the idea of reports aris-
ing'; but on the 9th she wrote 'Captain Graham came to dinner. We
got on very well, he told me his love affairs or rather the lack of
them.' By this time they were meeting nearly every day and Cairo
provided plenty of opportunities. There were the races ('Walked
nearly all the time with Captain Graham, lost my money but
enjoyed myself'), the polo, visits to the cavalry barracks ('Captain
Graham asked me to come into the garden, and we looked at everything, and then to his room, he was rather nice') and balls galore.
Finally at Madame d'Aubigny's dance she 'sat out nearly all the
time with my usual partner', and 'threw over Colonel Kitchener
(what a change!).'

There was one rather pathetic note in the midst of all this. She
was giving a tea-party at the hotel when suddenly Mr Scrutton,
who had fallen so much in love with her on board the *Austral*, was
announced. Presumably the class-conscious Radical felt himself out
of place among the diplomats and dashing cavalry officers, for Ellen
comments: 'It was rather awkward, for myself I was really pleased
to see him.' The next day he came to dinner. Perhaps she tried to
save him pain by putting him off, for she writes that a note of hers
miscarried. 'I saw him a moment alone. I wish he would forget me,
though it is nice to be cared for. We said good-bye, for good, I suppose.'

No such parting was in store for Captain Graham. On February
27th he came to tea and stayed to dinner, and 'then we went out
and sat in the moonlight. I was happy. All night nearly I couldn't
sleep. I felt so strange. He did love Lady Evelyn very much, but he
says he thinks God sent this to make it up to him.'

The next few days 'he' was naturally a frequent vsitor. 'He came
in the evening, it was heavenly'; though there is still a lurking unea-
siness about Lady Evelyn. (Beneath all her bounce Ellen throughout
her life suffered from an incurable diffidence – perhaps because she
had been so much snubbed in her youth.) 'In the evening he came as
usual, and we had a talk. It is only just over and I believe now only
because she isn't nice about it. She treated him badly, but still I
know he thinks it is over but I am not quite sure.' She really had no
cause for qualms. 'He said he did care for her but it is all right now.
We all wrote to Papa. I am waiting for him – and he came and we
sat in the garden – and – .'

The announcement caused great pleasure at home. Mary wrote:

Of course Papa wouldn't allow he was pleased till as he says he has made enquiries; but don't tell me. His blue eyes are all of a twinkle and he jokes and laughs about it and we are all of opinion he is pleased as Punch. Mama is delighted, and *so* nice about it, she quite cried with joy and we hugged one another over it, she wanted Papa to telegraph 'congratulations' but 'he must make enquiries' so don't expect to hear just yet, but take my word for it we are all delighted. I think and don't only think but know he is a *very lucky man* to get you and you are happy because you deserve it you always did what you thought was your duty and went straight ahead with it and if you made mistakes they were only mistakes.

Papa's letter came a fortnight later, and they were able to consider themselves 'properly engaged'. The next ten days, before Ellen sailed for home, passed in a welter of congratulations, taking of photographs, exchange of presents, all the usual paraphernalia of an engagement. This is always a strain on the nerves and there was a slight quarrel or two. They went several times to early service together, and there was a moonlight expedition to the Pyramids, which was recalled by Henry after she had gone home:

'Yesterday I rode out to the Pyramids, it was so different to the time when you and I dined there with Mrs Oswald and I had no one to sing little bits of songs and tell me what the stars and flowers thought on my way home. Do you remember that night? · I do, it was so nice.

Not many of Henry's letters survive. They include a good deal of dull everyday news, but it is amusing to see how they warm up. The first is signed: 'With all my love, yours ever Henry Graham', but two months later we have 'With my greatest love to my own, own darling pet.' Only one letter from Ellen seems to be extant though Henry thanks her for writing so often and says that her 'pretty letters' make him so happy when he receives them. The sole survivor seems to inject a slight note of doubt: 'Do you really think you will be happy for the rest of your life, my baby? *Perhaps.*'

Ellen left Egypt on March 25th, sailing in the *Paramatta*. Her first two visits on reaching home were to her dressmaker and to Doctor

Horsley. The latter pronounced Willy as being quite able 'to take care of himself now, it is such a relief, I *am* thankful.' Then there was a joyful reunion with the Surteeses and a 'real old gossip about old times, our journey, Captain Lambton etc.'

North Wales, as usual, proved something of a damper. Both her sisters' love affairs were in the doldrums. Aunt Margaret, who had been so kind to her and Willy, had died of cancer and when Papa came back from her funeral he was 'low and cross, and we were all late for dinner most unlucky!' Worst of all Willy had made advances to a Miss Frost; Ellen had to speak to him about it, 'and now Mama knows.'

It was presumably this peccadillo that inflamed Papa's temper and led him to turn his son and daughter out of the house.

> Papa gave Willy and me notice to quit this morning. Willy directly and I soon. He speaks most brutally about Willy, I think he has behaved most badly to him all the time, he never would realize his illness simply to save himself trouble.

Although Papa was profoundly dissatisfied with Willy and irritated by Ellen's championship of him, he was not really anxious to cut himself off from his favourite daughter. A few days later he was suggesting that Henry and Ellen might take Plas Ffron, a small country house between The Gerwyn and Cefn. 'He wants us to live there,' Ellen wrote, 'I *don't*.' She had never liked North Wales and perhaps the truth was that Papa had never liked it either. A letter which he wrote to her about this time shows, probably unconsciously, his disappointment with his own lot in life.

> Pray take your Father's advice, and defer to your husband as a wife should. Settle your fortune by all means – but let him have the practical disposal of it – and you will be much more likely to lead a happy life. [Ellen Palmer had certainly never deferred to her husband and the Palmers saw to it that her money was tied up on her children.] Let him whatever it may be have an *occupation* and lend yourself heart and soul to his advancement. Such is a woman's vocation.

This letter reveals Archy Peel as a deeply frustrated man. During his courtship he had spoken of ambition, the House of Commons, and his desire to lay his triumphs at Ellen Palmer's feet. It was very natural in a man of his antecedents but we never hear any more of it. He resigned himself to a country gentleman's life in North Wales, to hunting, to breeding horses, to doing some local county work and to writing occasional letters to *The Times*. It was perhaps this sense of wasted talent that made his temper so unusually ferocious.

It must have been satisfactory for Ellen to feel that in future she could be completely independent of Papa, but it is obvious that the thought of her coming marriage was beginning to weigh upon her. 'Nice letter from Cairo, I wish I felt differently sometimes, I don't feel anything as I ought and I know I am a fool to write it down.'

Back in London she saw a good deal of the Surteeses, and even indulged in a 'bearfight'. She met her new in-laws to be and wrote: 'They were very nice to me, I feel to have a lot of relations'; and she went to get her ring, Henry having written to the jeweller to provide the best that money could buy. It was a large dark sapphire set between two diamonds, and it was, as she wrote 'a beauty', but, she added, 'I feel as if I oughtn't to have had such a nice one.' Uncle Roger gave her £100 for a wedding present, and she spent '£90 on *under* linen, but it is lovely, night-gowns especially, I hope *he* will like them.'

The time marched inexorably on – Ascot and garden parties and regattas and parties to meet relations – till, on August 7th, Henry returned, 'it seems so strange to have him back.' There were five days in London, mostly spent with the Surteeses. On the 12th the engaged couple went down to North Wales and 'Papa met us at the station, and it was all very satisfactory.' Then came another visit to London with dressmakers and 'lots of shops'. Midge was 'low' (she never cared much for Henry Graham), and Captain Bourke 'said good-bye, and gave me a lovely travelling clock.' One wonders a little. He was well known as a devastating charmer and seems to have divided his attention between her and Midge.

On August 28th Ellen went up to North Wales, to be followed two days later by Henry and Midge. There was the presentation of a silver kettle from the parish and a clock from Bangor School. She was beginning to feel almost tearful. 'Last dinner in the oak room. Everybody is awfully kind, all the servants gave me presents, the cook was most touched, and everyone is so good.'

Then on September 2nd came the wedding in Bangor Church.

There were several triumphant arches, six bridesmaids, in white nun's veiling, with sleeves and sashes of white corded silk and white ostrich feather hats, and there was a page in a white satin Van Dyke costume. Papa, rather typically, insisted on starting too early and 'we had to go back which was trying. They played 'the Voice', 'the Church's One Foundation' etc. Lots of people came in the afternoon. We went to the Hand at Llangollen, and I – very much against my will – was married.'

'No other baby will ever be THAT baby'

Considering that Ellen had just had her twenty-seventh birthday, that in view of Willy's proclivities she had been forced into un-usually close proximity with the seamy side of sex, considering also the frank and uninhibited friendships she herself had had with men, the next entry in the diary is surprising and a little touching. 'I was awfully frightened and nearly fainted after dinner, He was too nice.'

The marriage between Henry Graham and Ellen Peel was a fail-ure. She was doubtful about it from the moment that she reached England. She was not in love with him and she knew it, but having once committed herself the outside pressures were so many and so varied that it would have been very hard to withstand them. Nevertheless the marriage might well have survived this incompata-bility of emotion. Marriages were more durable in those days. More-over Henry was affectionate, generous and warm-hearted, while she too was all these things. He loved her ardently, and if she could not reciprocate it, she was always passionately grateful for love; and she had the strongest possible sense of duty. But there was another factor which wrecked them. Papa should have been more careful in 'his enquiries'. Instead of haring off, as he did at one point, on a false trail which supposed old William Graham to have been a money-lender, he should have found out something about his future son-in-law's moral character, either from his family or from his reg-iment. For Ellen had no idea when she married him that Henry Graham was an alcoholic.

One cannot tell for certain when she first found out. Her diary from 1890 to 1892 gives little help. It is more and more a list of names and engagements, but it may have been about eight months after her marriage. There is a cryptic entry for May 6th 1891: 'Quarrelled with Henry and he told me.' She used that locution all through the diaries when the information was important and pri-vate and one cannot imagine what else it could have been. A fortnight later she recorded: 'Lizzie [Henry's married sister] told me all sorts of things and was very nice.'

Up to this time, and indeed after it, their married life had followed traditional patterns. They had taken a house at Aldershot, bought furniture, entertained, hunted and raced. There were a few minor rows. 'We came back with the plate chests, I was very cross & Henry was a sweet.' 'Had words with Henry. My fault.' And on at least two occasions 'Henry gave me a lecture.' There were domestic difficulties too. One cook got drunk, refused to go to bed and had to leave next morning. Characteristically Ellen commented: 'I was so sorry for her.' The next cook burst the boiler. There were difficulties with relations: younger brothers turned up unexpectedly demanding lunch. Henry's sisters were quarrelsome and sulky and Willy, as always, was a problem. He had invented a new sort of gun, which was to be strapped to the horse's belly in cavalry charges and discharged automatically, leaving the rider's hands free to control his mount. He was obsessed with this new ploy and even Ellen's patience began to wear a little thin. 'Willy lunched with us and was very rude to Henry about his bothering old gun.' One can see why. He presumably felt just like an elder child who sees his place taken by a newcomer, but it made things difficult for Ellen. 'I do wish he would be civil to people, Henry especially,' she wrote.

There were other family events. Papa and Mama decided to leave North Wales and to take a house in Hertfordshire, Westlea, near Broxbourne; and Mary at long last married Captain Fenwick and went to live at Plas Ffron, which Ellen had so decidedly rejected.

Then in June 1891 Ellen found herself pregnant. 'Have been to the doctor. It is.' Midge was also in the same state, and they renewed old memories by a little jaunt to Homburg. There they met the Prince of Wales 'who was most kind and nice to us both.' There is no mention in the diary of the fact that the Prince, who disliked the state of pregnancy, sent his equerry to inform them of this fact and to suggest that they might move somewhere else. This they resolutely refused to do, and it seems to have had no particular ill effects, for on their last day the Prince asked Midge to dine with him, 'but too late.' Ellen did add thoughtfully that perhaps it had been a mistake when, four years later, finding themselves in the same condition, they chose to revisit Homburg and met the Prince again.

Disapproval from the Prince of Wales was not the only drawback that pregnancy brought with it. At such a time women are often particularly subject to natural needs. In the nineteenth century however there were very few public conveniences and almost none for ladies. They solved the problem in the following way. Drawers in the 'nineties were made of very fine linen or batiste (silk was considered tarty and cotton was unthinkable); they had a draw string round the waist and a very large open vent between the legs. Stockings were frequently kept up by garters. It was therefore perfectly easy when standing in the prescribed attitude (one sees it in so many pictures of the 'nineties and the Edwardian era) leaning slightly forward, the hands clasped over the handle of the long parasol to urinate gently and imperceptibly on to the lawns of Hurlingham or the gardens of Homburg. It gave one, apparently, a curious sense of pleasure to carry on a conversation with a member of the opposite sex about politics or racing or gossip, while he remained totally unaware that all the time one was performing a most intimate and private function.

Nothing during this time denotes any problems to do with Henry's drinking. Probably with the optimism of youth and of her own nature she felt sure she could cure him. Surely his problem was not so bad as Willy's? She was becoming fonder of him. At Homburg she had written: 'Got a letter from Henry. I *do* miss him so'; and later in the year he took her on a quick trip to Paris, the South of France and Italy, which seems to have been a great success. She went sightseeing with all her usual energy though she must have been fairly large at the time, with her baby due in three months' time. It was tardy in arriving and she was alone at her mother-in-law's house in Sussex Square, since Henry had to remain with his regiment. The servants were surly, the butler drank, she was very large and she felt miserable. At last on Tuesday February 2nd at two o'clock in the morning the pains began. She had a horrible confinement. 'Henry stayed and held my hand, I wasn't brave a bit, quite the contrary, but the pain puts you out of your senses. They gave me a little laudanum, and chloroform at 12.30 and howked the baby out with instruments at half past three on Wednesday morning.' It had been a twenty-six-hour labour.

The baby made up for it. 'He was lovely, a boy with blue eyes, weighed 10 lb., I loved him when he came.' But he lived only five weeks. Ellen's milk failed and he could not take a bottle or to the wet-nurse they eventually found for him. He finally died in convulsions after much suffering. For the last time Ellen used her diary as a safety-valve for her emotions and wrote an account of those harrowing last days. It is very moving and one thing is noticeable in it: although her own grief was lacerating she thought not of herself but of the baby and what he had to undergo.

I prayed for his death the last poor mercy you can pray for your dearest, your own. They suffer and suffer and you cannot help, such a little tiny baby, and it is dumb and suffering, and you cannot even give it sympathy in its bitter trial though you would cut off your right hand to do so. It is bitter to part with him, it is hard to bear, but it is bitterer to see him suffer, and you cannot penetrate that wall that shuts him in, to suffer and to die.

Henry, she wrote, was very good to her; 'he put away his sorrow for me.' Midge and Mary wrote, and 'the love comforts me a little but it does not lessen the pain he had to bear.'

Her own pain continued. 'It is all over, never again shall I hold him in my arms, no other baby we may have will ever be *that* baby, with his lovely eyes that knew me.' When they came home after the funeral both she and Henry thought they heard the baby, and she dreamed every night that he was back in her bed, and woke, clasping the pillow.

She went down to Hythe to recuperate and after a week returned to Aldershot and the daily round. She was horrified to find that perhaps she was starting another child. 'I was so nervous I went to Dr Williams who said he didn't know!' She was quite right; she had another son in eight months' time. Her pregnancy and confinement were both easier and she grew to love him devotedly, as she did all her children, but 'no other baby will ever be *that* baby.'

After little Fergus's death the diaries stopped. There is a gap of thirteen years. Possibly she ceased writing, more probably she destroyed what she had written. She may have felt that this period of her life was too painful to recall; she may not have wished Henry Graham's two sons to read about it, for during this time their father's alcoholism got worse and worse. She battled valiantly for eight years but she was defeated. Things became steadily worse. Henry took to sleeping with a pistol under his pillow and he used to wake her up in the night and make faces at her. It was not only her own predicament, there were now two little boys to consider and Ellen, with what heart-searching we can only guess, separated from her husband in 1900. He went abroad, partly in hope of curing himself, partly with the idea of getting some sort of job behind the lines in South Africa (he had retired from the Army in 1899). For obvious reasons he did not succeed and after a while he ended up in a private home on the English south coast under the care of a nurse. The separation was a most amicable one. 'I can always trust you what to do for our sons,' he wrote; and she: 'Please don't bother about doing anything more for me about money. I expect I shall get on very well – and I daresay you are not too well off yourself.'

She was however lonely, and exceedingly unhappy. She used to walk down the Brompton Road looking at the sunsets, trying to obtain comfort from their beauty. She thought, perhaps not very seriously, of suicide, but she was sure she would never have the courage, and there were the two little boys. She wondered if the Roman Catholic Church could help her and went for instruction to the Brompton Oratory. Her teacher was one Father Sebastian, who had been a brother officer of Uncle Roger's in the Life Guards. He had been rather 'a rip' in his day, and his brother officers could never get over the idea of his being a priest. He was not, Ellen thought, a very good teacher (at all events he failed utterly to convert her) but he must have had a sense of humour. At the end of her instruction, after telling him that she could not become a Catholic, she asked him if, according to his creed, she must as a heretic go to Hell. 'Well,' he replied, 'you won't be able to plead invincible ignorance for I myself have taught you – but I think you may get away with invincible stupidity!'

Ellen was not only lonely, she was very badly off. Henry paid for the boys' schooling; for everything else she had to manage on her own money and a very small allowance from Uncle Roger. On this she had to keep herself, two children, a house, and three servants. In after life she used to marvel that she found three servants necessary; but it was a convention of the day, servants were cheap, houses were far from labour saving and no one in her milieu was brought up to do household tasks. No doubt she could have learned to do them, but she was able to solve her problem in a different way. She turned to account her undoubted talent for writing and she was soon a working journalist. She began writing articles for

The Onlooker, a glossy fashionable magazine with a more serious and cultural side to it. She wrote advertising copy and fashion notes with equal fluency (her editor was particularly delighted with her choice of headline for a slimming cure 'O that this too, too solid flesh would melt'); but she also tackled more serious subjects. She was not a suffragette but she reported suffragist meetings and speeches with intelligent interest, laying stress on the aspect that those who did not want the vote for themselves should consider the five million women workers 'often sweated and woefully underpaid' to whom it was a necessity.

The most serious contribution was a series of articles on the new religions, then springing up on every side. These included Revivalism and Spiritualism, but the three most important articles dealt with Christian Science. Even at this date they make interesting reading and the correspondence they evoked is more entertaining still. Mrs Hannah More Kohaus got exceedingly provoked when the irreverent Ellen quoted her picture of the Great Millennium, where, according to Mrs Kohaus, 'the Lion shall lie down with the Lamb and the Anaconda be coiled up in the Dove's nest.' 'Here, one cannot help feeling,' Ellen commented, 'that, though the two former may find their part in the programme convenient enough, the two latter will be less fortunate.' 'Had the writer's intellect been even partly illumined by spiritual insight,' riposted Mrs Kohaus 'there might have been one more soul over which to rejoice that "intellect" – the usurper – had been dethroned and a more worthy king ruling in its place.'

In addition to her journalistic work Ellen produced two novels, *The Tower of Siloam* and *The Disinherited of the Earth* which won some critical acclaim. *The Standard,* then one of the most influential of the book-reviewing papers, wrote of *The Tower of Siloam*:

It looks as though in Mrs Henry Graham a new author of considerable ability has just made her first bow to the public. There is a distinctly new note in *The Tower of Siloam*. The observation is quick and acute. The point of view is original. The writer has a cultivated style and can suggest repressed emotion without enumerating the heart throbs. In a phrase – and in spite of certain distinct crudities – Mrs Graham impresses one as a voice and not an echo of outworn platitudes and distant commonplaces.

Epilogue

Henry Graham died on February 13th 1907 and was buried at Twickenham next to his little son. Ellen had never broken off relations with him. She knew that he lived with the nurse who was in charge of him because one day when she was visiting him she went into his bedroom and saw the unmade bed with the impression of two heads on the pillow. She was glad, she felt it made him less lonely; and in the end the nurse cured him of drinking. 'I couldn't do it,' Ellen admitted, 'though I tried my best for years and he loved me dearly. But although he didn't care for her and she was as ugly as an old boot, she managed it.'

When she knew that he was cured Ellen wanted him to come back to her. It must have been a difficult decision to make. She had her own life, her writing, and already her friendship with George Askwith, but she was very fond of Henry and her sense of duty had always been unswerving. He was diffident at first. 'What would people say?' he asked. 'What does it matter what *anyone* says,' she replied robustly. 'This only concerns you and me.' He *was* so pleased,' she used to add in later days. So it was arranged, but it was not to be. Death intervened.

After Henry's death the regular diaries were resumed. Almost the first entry in March 1907 runs: 'Went to Twickenham with flowers. I felt calmer afterwards – but have and do feel it *so much*. I miss him so.'

Another equally, perhaps even more, pathetic entry is that for June 26th.

> Went to Hampstead. Saw poor Willy through the door. He looked horribly and unnaturally still, with his poor knees drawn up to keep off evil spirits and *one* eye shut – but they say he is not unhappy . . . He has grown a curly brown beard and looks like the Messiah . . . poor poor boy.

When and why Willy collapsed into total insanity is lost during those thirteen unchronicled years; but it almost seems as if Fate were pushing the previous major participants in her life into the wings, leaving the stage clear for a new leading character.

George Askwith boasted of an almost pure Yorkshire pedigree, descended from generation on generation of yeoman farmers. His father, however, had come south to take up a cadetship at Woolwich Academy. He had risen in his profession, become a general, married the sister of a brother officer with a little money, and never returned to Yorkshire. Of his five sons three followed him into the Army, one went into the Navy, and George, the cleverest, took First Class honours at Oxford before going to the Bar. He went into the chambers of Sir Henry James (the Attorney General, afterwards Lord James of Hereford) and became his right hand assistant, but his real talents were not for litigation but for arbitration. He handled one or two important arbitration cases for the Board of Trade and in August 1907 Lloyd George, the then President, asked him to join the Department as Assistant Secretary in charge of the railways. By the time he met Ellen Graham therefore he had set his foot on the ladder of the career that was to make his name.

We do not know exactly when or where they first met. They used to say that their first encounter had been at the house of a woman where they had never dined before and where they never dined again. George liked to add that the dining-room chairs were an uneven set and that he was given a very low one, so that though he was six foot and she was five foot four he had to look up to his partner!

His first extant letter to her is dated January 10th 1906, and though it is not exactly a love letter, it does show a great intimacy. He had received some very bad news (he does not say what, but it was probably financial, since this was always a problem) and he wrote:

> I should have gone nearly mad, but for your 2nd letter which I read several times. Possibly the best way is to put oneself outside circumstances – but then, but then, even then.
>
> Anyway, you were a dear and great comfort and you are dear,
>
> Yr. G.

They did not marry till two years after this letter and perhaps at one time they even contemplated having an affair, for once, discussing someone else's unhappy liaison, Ellen wrote: 'Do you remember I used to be afraid that if – we might come to that? But I knew I never could. I always want all or nothing and it's ridiculous to say you can't get it – because you can *always* choose nothing.'

Henry's death however left the way clear and by June 1907 they were already looking at houses. In those days a year's mourning was the absolute minimum. Anything else would have been considered grossly indecent. So although they were very deeply in love they waited. At this period George was perhaps the more carried away. For anyone who knew his deep inner reserve his love letters are astonishing. 'I was very late this morning,' he wrote to her one Sunday, 'because though I awoke at 7 I dozed or semi-dozed thinking of you for about 2 hours – all on end – & just you and nothing else – your talk, your mind, your aura, your hair, your form – YOU.'

Her letter is also written on a Sunday. Both are undated (common form for her, unusual for him) but they are about the same period and they may even have crossed.

I am *so* looking forward to our life together. Sometimes it seems as if I were the happiest woman in the world. It's what I have always wanted besides – I could never *really* have cared about a man (at least I don't mean that – but I should always have regretted it) who had not a work to do that was worth doing and that he *really* cared about, heart and soul – And we do get on together well, don't we? *Unberufen*, very *unberufen*!! – but I *am* happy – and I *will* say it – It makes me just long that everyone should be happy too. I wish one could scatter it about, like sunshine – and especially on you – dearest – I hope I will. I do hope so, & pray so. I am going to church to pray about it now.

From first to last, as this letter shows, her concern for and admiration for his work were passionate and absorbing. When in August 1907 he was suddenly sent for to Belfast, at the urgent request of Sir Anthony MacDonnell, the Permanent Under-Secretary of State, to settle what seemed an almost insoluble dock strike escalating into bloodshed, she wrote as follows:

What terrible news from Belfast last night – I do hope you

won't get into any danger. Please buy *all* the papers & send them to me – couldn't you give an order for the daily paper if there is one – to be sent to me as long as it lasts? It will be glory if it all goes right . . . I am so excited about it all. I feel this is your great chance – and I simply *pray* that they will – and listen – and I *know* you will do it so well. *Don't* forget to send me every scrap of news about it.

Against all odds her prayers were answered. The leader of the strike was James Larkin, a fiercely intransigent militant who preached class warfare. George went down to the strike leader's bare little office in the docks and waited, perched on a table since there were no chairs, till Larkin came in. Somehow, by exercising his almost magnetic influence, he induced Larkin to formulate his claims and to meet with the employers. He found time to keep Ellen informed of all stages of the negotiations. He described the soldiers in the side streets sitting 'on tea chests and bags of sugar' in the grocers' shops. He told her of the moment when the talks nearly broke down when the employers' representative said he would not be threatened and would withdraw. 'Sir Anthony banged the table and nearly ordered him to the door. I coldly remarked we were discussing a very narrow issue and it seemed to me we had better keep our tempers.' Finally a settlement was reached and George accompanied Larkin to the men's mass meeting.

1,000 of them, great rough fellows in caps who had been waiting three hours, and listened with the most intense interest to every word. Speeches explained everything, and then a storm of questions, which were adroitly answered by the leaders, who from time to time turned to me to assist them. Finally it was passed *unanimously* – amid a storm of cheers . . . Then there were votes and cheers for Sir A. – and then for me, and I was called on for a speech. I made a short one and they rose at me. They yelled and cheered and clappped and flung their caps in the air, and yelled again, and cheered till I thought they would never stop. Have you ever felt a real lump in your throat, not knowing whether to laugh or cry? I did then, I confess.

It was an euphoric moment, but the rejoicings could not go on for ever. The close of his letter paints a more sombre picture.

At any moment now another row may occur, and they are doubtful how many troops they can take away – The millers (Protestants) are threatening to strike because the carters (Catholics) have got something, and the city is suspicious and in the bye streets there is seething discontent. 181 persons killed or wounded is the secret story – 200 *tons* of cobble stones taken away from the heaps prepared to stone the soldiers – (the whole city is to be paved with *flags* as soon as possible) – & damage, heaven knows to what value, by loss of trade, no visitors, empty hotels, no wages, ships not coming etc. etc. People say it will take 20 years to recover.

The back of the strike was broken but George had to stay on in Ireland for another ten days formulating a tariff for wages which it was hoped would stick, consolidating the 'various agreements and anomalies of the coal-porters' and coal-carters' wages and conditions'. It was always a part of his policy not to leave the scene of a dispute until he had 'made a start with better "machinery" for the future.' When at last he did get away he went for a well-earned holiday, yachting with Lord Dunraven off the southern coast of Ireland. Ellen was with her boys up in North Wales, and there are several letters belonging to this period which show how much their separation cost them. In one he tells her that he has visited the Convent of the Poor Clares, where they made lace, and talked to

such a dear old abbess all about her work, and her reclamations from savagery and her wages to the workers and her lace. She was so pleased and such a dear old thing. I bowed to her and kissed her hand at parting and she cried. She liked someone who appreciated lace I think. [He must have learned about it settling the Nottingham lace piece rates in 1905.] I got a little piece for you, I tried to get it good, though small, and that you might wear it with anything, and got the technical description with it.

She answered, 'The abbess must have been a darling. I am so glad you pleased her. There are wonderful women hidden away in corners of the world. I know I shall love the lace.'

Ellen was up in North Wales staying with Mary and George Fenwick when the lace arrived. A day or two later she talked to Uncle Roger 'about my future, and he was very nice.' The diary is disappointingly uncommunicative about what effect her news had on the rest of her family. She was now on better terms with her parents. Basically she had always loved and admired Papa and Mama had been affectionate and helpful when the baby died. They may not have been best pleased about her marriage. George's career was only just taking off, he had no money and though his background was sound upper middle class, he had no aristocratic connexions like the Peels or the Russells. By this time. however, they must have realized that Ellen knew her own mind. For her part she was only sorry for the rest of the world that did not share her own good fortune.

He lives in a box [she wrote to George, describing Uncle Roger]. 'Fast bound in misery and iron', I always think of him, poor old dear, when I read that text. And one wants to get through to him – and one can't – the bars are too strong. It is all so sad. He is old and unhappy and he has missed the way, he has not found the House Beautiful – that's nothing, lots of people don't – but he has never even seen it – nor Milly either. They haven't got the proper values of things, and they are *so* poor with all their money. I feel so dreadfully sorry for them sometimes. And when I think of *us* and all our happiness. You are going to take me to the House Beautiful – you have already – and besides that I have the boys, who are dears and love me – and you have your work which is so much to both of us – and enough money and good health – it seems almost too much happiness. I want to shower it on everybody and take them to the golden country too. I do so wish that everybody else was happy too, don't you?

On this characteristic note Ellen Graham got married, on February 20th 1908, from her father's house, Westlea. George, rather typically (he was always bad at practical arrangements), nearly missed his own wedding owing to a puncture in the then new-fangled motor car. Ellen, even more typically, confessed in her thank-you letter to Mama that she had left behind her silver-headed umbrella and the Bramah key of her jewel case. They caught the train by a whisker. Lord James of Hereford had lent them his house, Breamore, for the honeymoon and there they passed the next three weeks; the first four days of which are grouped by Ellen in her diary under the simple inscription: 'In Heaven'.